#2SIDES

#2SIDES
MY AUTOBIOGRAPHY

RIO FERDINAND

The Five Mile Press Pty Ltd
1 Centre Road, Scoresby
Victoria 3179 Australia
www.fivemile.com.au

Part of the Bonnier Publishing Group
www.bonnierpublishing.com

Copyright © Rio Ferdinand, 2014
Text written by David Winner, 2014
Text copyright © Blink Publishing, 2014
All rights reserved. No part of this book may be reproduced, stored in a retrieval system, or transmitted by any form or by any means, electronic, mechanical, photocopying, recording or otherwise, without the prior written permission of the publisher.

First published by Blink Publishing, 2014
This edition published in 2014 by The Five Mile Press Pty Ltd

Printed in Australia at Griffin Press.
Only wood grown from sustainable regrowth forests is used in the manufacture of paper found in this book.

Typeset by Fakenham Prepress Solutions
All images © Rio Ferdinand unless otherwise stated
Design by www.envydesign.co.uk

Every reasonable effort has been made to trace copyright holders of material reproduced in this book, but if any have been inadvertently overlooked the publishers would be glad to hear from them.

Acknowledgements

I would like to thank my wife Rebecca for her ongoing support with my football career and off-the-field projects – you have been a rock. My children Tia, Lorenz and Tate for making me smile. My father Julian and his partner Lisa, my mother Janice and her partner Peter for their unconditional love and support, my brothers Anton and Jeremiah, my sisters, Sian, Chloe, Anya, Remy and everyone who has played a part in helping me to get to this point in my life; you have all played your part, thank you, love always.

I would to say a big thank you to Sir Alex Ferguson who has been a great manager and inspiration to me, Harry Redknapp who gave me my first opportunity in football, all the coaches, physios, kit men, and canteen staff that have looked after me throughout my career. Thank you.

A big thank you to all the players I have played with over the years – too many to mention – it has been amazing. Thank you to all the players I have played against and kept me on my toes, thank you!

A special thanks to the fans, the rock of all football clubs, you have been a pleasure to work for and I thank you for that.

ACKNOWLEDGEMENTS

I would also like to give a big thank you to Pini Zahavi, Jamie Moralee, Pete Smith and all the staff at New Era Global Sports Management who have been the catalyst behind helping me prepare for life after football, supporting and guiding me through my football career and being there for me through the good and the bad times.

Thank you all
Rio, July 2014

Foreword

I always said when Rio was a skinny 16-year-old wonderkid at West Ham that he would go right to the very top – and he did.

What a player he's been! He fulfilled all his early promise and made himself a fantastic player – the best defender in Europe without a doubt.

A Rolls-Royce on the field, he was always a smashing guy off it as well.

He began his career as a player with me at West Ham and I'm so happy we've been able to hook up together again at QPR.

But there's more to Rio than a great footballer.

He comes from a lovely family and, as this unusual, honest and thoughtful book shows, he's matured into a remarkable man: intelligent, decent and with lots to say about football and life.

It'll be a sad day when he finally hangs up his boots, but I'll make another prediction. Whatever he does next will be worth watching too!

Harry Redknapp

Contents

Acknowledgements	v
Foreword	vii
Respect	1
On Defending	11
Relentless	23
Back Story	33
On Racism	45
England: Hoddle and Co.	73
Moscow, 21st May 2008	85
Sir Alex Ferguson	91
Wildebeest	103
On Balance	107
Barça	111
On Gay Footballers	119
On Being Captain	123
The Nice Guy	127
On Pressure and Boredom	149
Roy Keane	155
Black Coaches	161

CONTENTS

My Week and My Music	165
Trash Talkers	175
Outside Interests	181
Paul Scholes	189
Frankly	193
5.7 Million and Counting	203
Wayne Rooney	211
Mums and Dads	215
Ronnie and Leo	221
My Foundation	229
Life After Football	235
World Cup 2014	243
Coming Home	257
Index	265

Respect

I played on the estate for fun
But those guys
If they saw me on the street
If they said 'That's Rio
He's a good footballer'
That's all I wanted people to say

Between the two blocks of my building on the estate there was a little green. It was crap. But it was fantastic. It was our Wembley, our Old Trafford. When you played football there you had to avoid the trees and make sure you didn't twist your ankle in any of the holes in the ground. We didn't have the sort of nice goals with nets that kids have today. One goal was a tree; the other would be someone's jumper. Sometimes we'd play three- or four-a-side. Sometimes it was 15-a-side. It all depended who was around. I didn't like playing with kids my age because I found their games childish. I preferred playing football with the older boys. Normally they'd have said I was too young, but they respected me because I was good at football and let me join in. We used to sit on the stairs and laugh and chat about the game and life until late at night. They were good players too, and Liverpool fans mostly. One of them, Gavin Rose, was two years older than me, and better than I was. We called him 'our John Barnes.' He's still my best friend.

My Dad didn't care much for football. He was more into kung fu. But I played every day, every weekend, every hour. After school I'd be outside messing about with skills, or kicking about on the estate. There was nothing else going on. It was all quite natural and rustic. We might have been on a council estate in south London but our outlook was international. A guy called Stefan had all the latest videos from Serie A in Italy, which was the best league in the world at the time. So we'd troop over to Stefan's house, watch Italian football then go out and try to replicate what we'd seen. The entire world of football wasn't available to us at the touch of a button via satellite, cable and the internet like today. But we watched everything we could on TV, with programmes like *Match of the Day*, *Grandstand* and *Saint and Greavsie*.

These days my son, before he goes to bed, will say, 'Dad, can you put on that YouTube video of Neymar please?' Back then, my hero was Maradona. I loved Stefan's videos of him doing keepy-uppies and playing in the World Youth Championships with Argentina. The way he took people on and ran past them was just fantastic. When we played, we all wanted to be Maradona and we'd do the radio commentary of the goal he scored against England. You'd be dribbling and shouting it out: 'He turns like an eel, the little squat man ...' (we knew it by heart) '... He comes inside Butcher, leaves

RESPECT

him for dead ... outside Fenwick, leaves *him* for dead ...' Then I'd score by hitting the tree ... 'And that's why Rio is the *greatest player in the world!*'

Maradona was the first person I thought 'I'd love to be like that guy.' But physically I could hardly have been more different. As I got older I started liking other players like Frank Rijkaard, John Barnes, Paul Ince and Gazza. If someone was just a runner or kicked people, they weren't for me. I liked the flair players – we all did. John Barnes was the best-loved English player. But mostly we admired the foreign stars, and worked on our technique. Whoever produced the best bit of skill was considered the main man on the estate.

It was only much later, when I trained at various clubs, that I realised skill wasn't exactly the quality most appreciated in the English game. I was so lucky, especially at West Ham, that I had coaches who never tried to brainwash me into a different way of playing. They embraced my style and wanted you to keep your own identity. A lot of the West Ham players who came through around that time have a touch of flair: Glen Johnson is not your typical right back; Michael Carrick's got great feet, great class, vision, range of passing; Joe Cole, especially when he was a kid, was an incredible skill man; Frank Lampard was always his own man. We were never forced to play a certain way; nobody ever shouted 'get rid' at us.

When I was about 13, Gavin had the idea of going over to Burgess Park on Sundays to play with some much older African guys. They were from places like Sierra Leone and Nigeria, and they were tough and aggressive, and terrific footballers. My Mum didn't want me to go: she thought we'd get into trouble and if something kicked off, we'd either have to stand and have a fight, or run very fast to get away. Mum eventually came round, but the first few times I actually sneaked off the estate to go. To get to the park, we had to walk from the Friary Estate through two other estates, which was tricky in itself. Then we had to cross a bit of wasteland, a gypsy caravan site where there were big dogs roaming about which could be a problem especially when it got late.

The African guys were hard bastards and about twice our age – in their 20s and 30s. They turned up in cars and probably had families. We were of no interest to them at all, so we had to kind of force our way in. By this time, I'd already begun to think I could make it as a professional. But my motivation was always the same: I played for respect. Respect from your peers, respect from your opponents and your teammates, and respect from the people watching.

Anyway, my mates and me would go over to the park and just kick a ball about and try and show off our skills, hoping they would want us to join in. At first we'd ask and they'd say, 'no, you're too young.'

Then one time they let us play and realised we were quite good. After that they used to let us play all the time. Playing on my estate was fun; this was something else. These guys were quick and strong, and your own teammates would kick you if you didn't pass the ball. We never wore shin pads and when you got hacked down, which was often, it hurt and you'd want to cry. But you saw how they looked at you and

RESPECT

realised that if you started crying they wouldn't let you play again, so you had to just get through it any way you could.

These guys were much taller, quicker, bigger and stronger than me. I reckoned if I could play with them, I would be doing well, I learned to pass and move with a bit more thought. It wasn't a great standard and there were no tactics to speak of. But physically and emotionally it was demanding. I couldn't outrun or out-muscle any of these guys so I had to try different things and work out ways of getting by people without just using my speed.

Playing there really helped me mature as a player but the funny thing is we never got to know any of them. If you ask me any of their names I wouldn't be able to tell you. We had a purely football relationship. We'd turn up on a Sunday, play for a few hours, and then go. They weren't interested in hanging out with teenagers. But when the game was finished I could walk away knowing I'd won their respect. If I was walking around anywhere and they saw me, they could say, 'Oh, that's Rio, he's a good footballer.' That's all we wanted people to say.

I really worry that youngsters coming into football today are overprotected. Compared to the generations of players who went before, they're treated with kid gloves and surrounded by cotton wool. But when things get difficult in their careers or in their lives they may struggle.

One of the big differences between now and when I was a kid is that they now get ferried to and from training by car. Everything is done for them. When I was 14, I had to make two-hour journeys by buses and trains just to get to and from training. After school, most of my mates just wanted to play spin the bottle and snog birds, so they made fun of me when I said 'I'll play for ten minutes but then I've got to go. I ain't missing my trains.' But there was no way I was going be late. Some of those guys were good enough to have played football professionally. But they were the ones who said: 'That bird's alright over there' and stayed. Now they're working on building sites.

This was the journey: from Blackheath Bluecoats, my school, I'd take a 53 bus to New Cross. That was 20-minutes. From New Cross I'd take the East London line to Whitechapel, then walk through to Bank and get the tube to Stratford from where I caught an overground train to Dagenham and Redbridge. Then it was another bus to Chadwell Heath and then a 10-minute walk to the West Ham training ground. And then the same back. We'd do that every Tuesday and Thursday night. There were three of us who did that every week from Peckham: Me, Andy McFarlane who's now a football agent and a good mate called Justin Bowen who still plays amateur football but works a normal job. It was a tough schedule, but it helped to make me the person I am. To make it, you had to have discipline and desire. I was moving in an adult world and learning to duck and dive.

The hardships of being an apprentice also tended to make you resourceful and resilient. Twenty years ago cleaning boots was part and parcel of becoming a professional footballer. On one of my first days at West Ham as an apprentice I was drilled by Tony Cottee; he was one of the club's best players at the time, the number nine, and one of my tasks was to take care of his boots. I remember being in the boot room, savouring the smell of dubbin and having a laugh, giving it loads of banter when I heard someone shouting my name: 'where's that fucking Ferdinand?' I came out and saw this five-foot-nothing stocky geezer standing there. Tony Cottee.

'Where's my fucking boots?' he said.

'What boots?' I said.

'You're my boot boy. Where's my boots?' he said.

I said they were hanging on his peg in the boot room where I'd been told to put them. He said: 'I want my boots with my training kit, wet top and track suit in my place every morning.' When I said that wasn't my job, he got angry: 'You're my boot boy and you'll do what I fucking say.' And then he walked off.

So every day that year Tony Cottee had *everything* just exactly the way he wanted, because that's the way it was.

That sort of thing is unimaginable now. Apprenticeships have gone. Aspiring stars don't get chapped fingers because it's freezing and they're outside having to scrub the mud off a pair of senior player's boots. I used to have to clean the away changing room and teams used to take as long as they liked. You'd poke your head round the door and say, 'can I come in now? I'm going to miss my train home.' And they'd say: 'Fuck off! Get out!' Every day there were these problems and little things you had to deal with. But dealing with them made you a little streetwise and sharp.

One of the worst jobs was to clean the toilets and you'd do anything to avoid that. So you'd do extra training and when someone challenged you you'd say 'I can't. I've got special training.' I was like Del Boy finding ways to use football to get out of horrible jobs. Frank Lampard and Joe Keith used to play games together all the time to avoid the nasty jobs. When Tony Carr, the youth team manager, told us to sweep floors, we'd say 'OK, but if our shooting and passing is rubbish on Saturday it'll be your fault.'

Where we had to *earn* privileges, young players today get them automatically. I think there's a downside to that.

For example, first team changing rooms used to be no-go zones for any young player. You had to really prove yourself before you went in there. Nowadays it's almost nothing. Adnan Januzaj was in the United changing room from day one as if it was completely normal – which for him it was. It's not his fault. He didn't know there used to be all these little staging posts during the course of a long career. You used to have to climb the ladder slowly. But society changed. I talked with Ji-Sung Park about how things were done in South Korea. 'The young players can't eat until the older players have eaten,' he said. 'They're not even allowed to sit down until the older players have been in and eaten.' I was like: 'Quite right!' But here things are all heading the other way.

There was a telling little incident with the exercise bikes at United. There's a row of bikes for the whole squad to use before training but it's understood that every first-team player has a particular bike they normally sit on. We all went down there after a meeting and one of the youth players is on Juan Mata's bike. 'Hey, that's Juan's bike.'

Then the youth team player looks at another youth team player as if to say: 'I'm not moving.'

I don't know if it was banter, but back in the day that was an immediate slap. 'You what?' Bang! 'Off that bike *now!*' But do that these days and you'll get reported and probably end up in the paper. Quietly someone told the lad: 'next time you see a first-team player coming and it's their bike you get off the fucking bike, right?'

Last season I was told that one of the United youngsters had cried in front of the manager. I asked what the matter was. 'I thought I was going to play today,' he explained. I reminded the player he was 19 years old and told him to stop crying like a little baby. Getting angry about not getting picked? Fair enough. But *crying* to the *manager* about not getting picked? It's mad.

Of course, plenty of kids are going to come through and do well anyway. But some other kids need to keep their feet on the ground, stay humble, and toughen up a bit as personalities and people. It will put them in good stead for the future and for what they're going to come across in their career. They might not make it at Manchester United. They may have to go back down to Bournemouth or Yeovil or Carlisle. And down there, if you're not hard enough, you'll get eaten alive because those guys are fighting for their lives. They're struggling. It's an entirely different environment.

Then there's the problem of money. It's not just that young players are getting huge amounts before they've proved themselves. Some are paid so much they think they've made it before they've even got off the bloody training pitch, and a lot of young players just want to be rich. It's a hard mentality for me to get my head round. For me the game was always about glory and winning and achieving things as a player. If you're successful you're going to be rich in most fields. But that's a side effect. Money has truly never been an issue for me.

When I was a kid I sometimes went to QPR games with my Dad – and I insisted we arrive early. Why? Because I wanted to see the pre-match warm-up. To me, the warm-up was better than the game because I'd see Ray Wilkins practising long passes. He'd hit beautiful balls down the line and I'd think: 'the ball doesn't make that sound when I kick it.' I'd then go home and practise and try to make the sound Ray Wilkins made. But I could never do it so I had all these questions. Does he strike the ball differently from me? Are we using a wrong ball? Is it because my boots aren't kangaroo skin? Nowadays kids come home from a game where they've seen a great player and they ask different questions.

'What car did he leave in?'

'What colour was it?'

'Was it a Ferrari?'

On Defending

He smelled one type of danger
I smelled a different type of danger

One day at West Ham our centre-halves didn't turn up for a game so the manager turned to me and said, 'Could you just play there this week?' I was about 15 at the time and my position was central midfielder, but fair enough. I did as he asked. I must have played well because after the game he said, 'Listen; I want you to play there next week, too.' I wasn't happy about that! In fact every time he asked me to play at the back I'd have a sulk about it. Soon it was all the time. I suppose defending came naturally to me but it certainly wasn't a pleasure. What I liked was dribbling and passing and shooting and scoring goals … and here I was stuck having to win the ball then give it to other people to do all that stuff!

I had a strangely unfulfilled feeling after games, even when we won. I thought: 'Yeah but I didn't do anything.' All I did was stop other guys scoring. Where's the fun in that? It carried on like that for years. In fact, all through the entire early part of my career I got no buzz out of blocking shots or breaking up goalscoring opportunities. I liked doing bits of skill or a good pass, or running with the ball. Admittedly, I did enjoy racing against a forward and beating him for speed. But the art of defending just left me cold. Even playing for England I still wasn't actually *enjoying* defending. If my team lost I wouldn't be too upset as long as I'd 'done something' in the game. I'd go home to my estate and watch *Match of the Day* with my mates and say: 'did you see my bit of skill?' I'd be proud of some trick or something I'd done against Alan Shearer, say, and wouldn't think about the fact that he'd scored a goal or got behind me.

It wasn't until I went to Leeds that my attitude began to change and mature – and my game really started to improve. I have to thank David O'Leary, the Leeds manager, for helping me. When I decided to leave West Ham, Chelsea wanted me but I realised I needed to leave London. I had to get away from the bright lights and all the invitations to nightclubs I found so hard to refuse. When I met the chairman, Peter Ridsdale, he talked about money and I wasn't listening. I was sitting there thinking, I don't really care about the money. I'm sure it will be more than enough. All I want to know is will David O'Leary make me a better player? I said, 'Listen, Mr Ridsdale, with all due respect, I'd rather just speak to the manager please.' So I did and I asked him what he had in mind. What did he see in me? Where could I improve? And all his answers were what I wanted to hear. He promised to make me a better footballer. He was saying things like: 'I want you to work harder, I won't give you any easy stuff. You'll work extra after training. You need to improve your heading and your concentration and the way you approach games.'

ON DEFENDING

A key moment came when I got injured in the first minutes of an FA Cup game against Cardiff. One of their players went over the ball and twisted my ankle. In truth, the damage was done before the match. A few of the lads had sawn Paul Robinson's shoes in half, and were generally messing around. It was just a stupid bit of banter while we were having a laugh in the changing room. When I got hurt on the field the manager told me it was my own fault. He said: 'You got injured because you were messing about before.' He explained that I had to go into games with my mind right, ready and focused, respecting your opponents. He said I couldn't expect to just switch my concentration on and off like a light bulb. I had to prepare long before the game. It was a breakthrough moment for me.

I always looked forward to playing against the best players. If I was facing Michael Owen, I'd be thinking, 'Let's see how quick he really is, I can't wait to race him.' I wanted to test myself against Dion Dublin or Les Ferdinand or Duncan Ferguson, who were all good and aggressive in the air. So I'd go into those games excited. The bigger the game, the higher the reputation of my opponent, the better I liked it.

But I still had a lot to learn – as I discovered during the World Cup quarter-final against Brazil in Shizuoka in Japan. For one thing, I went into the game with far too much emotion. Brazil was the international team I always supported after England; I loved them. So to play for England against Rivaldo and Ronaldo, who were the best players in the world at that time, was a dream. Added to that, all my friends and family were there. I could hear Mum shouting 'Rio, Rio' and I knew my Dad, brothers, sisters and my girlfriend Rebecca were all in the stadium, and … well, it just all got too much for me. As the national anthem played, I started welling up. I was way too emotional and, as a result, the game kind of passed me by and I didn't impose myself as I should have done.

That was a really important lesson. Ever since then I've made it a rule never to let that happen again. Don't get emotionally involved, don't get caught up in the atmosphere or the game will pass you by. You just have to shut off from everything. The moment you start hearing what the fans are shouting you think 'Woah, I'm not in the game, I'm not in the right frame of mind here' and concentrate harder. Of course, there are times when you just can't get into that mode but sometimes the game takes care of that for you. The intensity can force you to concentrate, or maybe you'll have a battle with someone, or you can talk yourself back into the right frame of mind.

That Brazil game taught me another lesson too. There was a moment of brilliance between Rivaldo and Ronaldo that left me open-mouthed. You can still see it on YouTube. Ronaldo was in the inside left channel just outside the box and played the ball to Rivaldo, then went towards the goal for a one-two. Naturally, I turned and, head down, sprinted towards goal because I thought this was going to be a race between him and me. But he'd sold me a dummy! He'd started to run, then checked, and gone back for the one-two to feet. While I was running towards goal like an idiot, he's

ON DEFENDING

gone back and made himself space for a free shot. I thought 'Bloody hell! That's different to anything I'm used to!' And that's when I thought I've still got loads of work to do if I'm going to be a world-class defender. But I loved that trick because it showed me the next level. It made me think, I need to do more. I've always learned more when I've failed at something. That's where a big chunk of my character has come from. The idea of being comfortable and satisfied with any achievements always scared me, because if I became satisfied, my foot would come off the gas, my standards would drop and success would dry up.

You're always learning and developing. I remember Frank Burrows, the reserve team manager at West Ham when I was growing up, always telling me to talk to the players in front of me in a game: 'You've got to talk to them, push them around, make your life easier.' At one level I understood what he was saying but I couldn't do it as a young player. It didn't help that I never felt I was an out-and-out defender. If we were losing they'd always put me up front to score a goal. So I still had an attacking frame of mind. More importantly, at that age I didn't concentrate well enough, and I didn't know when or where or how to give instructions.

My game improved a lot at Leeds because I was playing and training with better players and, being out of London, I had time to kind of think about the game a bit more and a bit deeper. But somehow, after that World Cup, it all just clicked into place. I don't know why, but I suddenly got it: this is a serious business and I need to make sure that everything's on point. And that's when I naturally started talking and moving people about on the pitch. Later at Man United, Nicky Butt even complained 'fucking hell, man, all I can hear is you shouting at me left, right, left, right!' He was kidding of course. People like Nicky and Owen Hargreaves told me I started making their lives much easier by talking. They didn't have to look around for people so much because I was telling them who to mark, when to block off a pass or whatever. People really started to put their confidence in me. I'd kind of blossomed and it all came together. Ever since, talking and organising people on the pitch has been an important part of my game. Paul Scholes or Michael Carrick or Giggsy or Darren Fletcher or anyone who's played in front of me will tell you that all they can hear in training or in games is me screaming and shouting. And of course helping them helped me.

It took me a while to adapt to United when I arrived from Leeds. The first training session is when you're most anxious. The most nerve-wracking thing isn't when you go out and play in front of tens of thousands in the stadium – it's when you go to the training ground and are training for the first time in front of your new teammates. You want to gain respect and show them that you are good enough to be there. At first I made the mistake of playing cautiously, making sure I didn't make a mistake. In training one time, I passed an easy square ball to Gary Neville and Roy Keane just ripped into me. He said: 'Listen; stop fucking playing safe, play the ball forward, you're not at fucking West Ham or Leeds now. Fucking play the ball forward.' My first reaction was: 'why's he attacking me? I've passed the ball to a teammate, I haven't given it away.' But, thinking about it, he was right: we were there to win, not coast. You've got to take risks if you're going to win.

There were loads of things like that to work on: I had to reach their higher level. It was a question of pushing, developing and growing all the time, testing yourself, stretching. Some people might go into their shells but I've always embraced challenges so, in a way, it was perfect for me. The sheer quality of that squad improved me. I was training against Ruud van Nistelrooy, Louis Saha; Ole Gunnar Solskjaer, Ryan Giggs, David Beckham. Later it was people like Rooney and Cristiano Ronaldo. You either sink or swim when you're in the water with people like that. My professionalism had to go up because I couldn't risk getting embarrassed. So my clubbing days had to be over immediately. I still went out. Don't get me wrong. But only at the right times.

Meanwhile, David James introduced me to a brilliant sports psychologist called Keith Power. I only had about a dozen sessions with him but he changed the way I approached games. One crucial thing he taught me was visualisation. I started preparing myself mentally days before a game. I'd see my first header, my first tackle, my first pass, my first run down a channel against my opponent. When these things came up in the game, it was already in my mind and I knew what to do. The morning of a match I'd do the same thing. And it really worked. For example, I'd see myself in a stadium playing against Raul. He's left footed and I know he likes to come in on his left foot, so I'd picture him getting the ball, turning, shooting with his left … and me blocking the shot.

Or I'd see myself going up for my first header against Kevin Davies ... and winning that ball.

Mostly, though, I improved because I was testing myself every day against fantastic players. Louis Saha was one of the hardest to play against. He'd be stepping on your toes, shooting off either foot; he was quicker than anyone else. What made him even harder to face was his opposite movement, meaning he'd run for the ball, then run behind you. And Scholesy would see him every time and put the ball on a sixpence for him. That was ridiculously hard to deal with. Louis was fantastic. I'm convinced that if he hadn't had injuries, he'd have been a top, top player. It was all good experience and I learnt so many lessons. The intensity was always higher than at my previous clubs. And the will to win was ferocious. In training, you absolutely had to win your individual battles because everyone had a big ego. When you arrived at Carrington, you'd hear the chatter. If someone got nutmegged he became an object of ridicule. You did NOT want to be the guy everyone was laughing at! So there was always something to play for. The players pushed each other to improve, and if we slackened Alex Ferguson or Carlos Queiroz would step in. One time we were doing a positional drill and it was wasn't as intense as it should have been. So Carlos stopped the training and was sharp with us: 'if you don't want to train, go inside. Do it properly.' We didn't like him sometimes because he used to get on our nerves. The training could be boring. But we really missed him when he left. He was one of the best coaches I worked with because he had such a clear picture of how he wanted you to play.

ON DEFENDING

When I was younger at West Ham, I was always quicker than any forward I played against. So, when the other team had the ball, or one of their midfielders or forwards was making a run, I used to say to myself: 'I'll give this guy a yard, then race him, beat him and then get the applause.' When I started playing in Europe I had to change. The ball comes in quicker, opponents identify space quicker, get their heads up quicker and pass the ball quicker. More importantly, if they get in on goal they don't need extra touches to get the ball under control. They take one touch then ... bang! You have no time to recover. So I learned to stay goal side. I couldn't rely on my pace because I'd get caught out at the highest level.

Whatever stage you are at in your career you have to keep learning and developing and solving new problems. When I was a kid with West Ham I'd be facing a certain type of forward, then you get into the first team and there's bigger, stronger people to deal with. Guys like Mark Hughes and Les Ferdinand could roll you, use their strength to ease you out of the way and then they're facing your goal with the ball and you're on the floor. So, I had to read situations like that. Sometimes I'd tap someone on one side of his body when the ball's coming in, so they think I'm coming that side, then go round the other. You'd be working to get little things like that in your game all the time. Neil Ruddock used to say to me, 'Go down their back with your studs from the first header when the ball goes up.' So sometimes the ball goes up, the referee's watching the ball, and you jump with your leading leg, and you put your studs down their back.

And then sometimes, the striker won't come near you for the rest of the game. Sometimes you do stuff like that if you're having a hard game. You try and do something a bit cute and hope the referee won't see it, just so that forward recognises that you're not messing about. But I'm not one for blood and thunder and lots of flying around. I always relied on being a bit smart, trying to do things a little bit differently to get the upper hand.

I played with a lot of fine players but I have to say my best defensive partner was Nemanja Vidić. One of the things that brought us together was that we were both highly competitive and determined to be the best. We shared a lot of ideas and ideals. He'd had a hard time when he first arrived. He came mid-season and people were saying: 'who is this guy? He's not ready to play for Man United.' He had a lot to prove over his first year or so. It was a big step up coming from the Russian league, to training against the likes of Rooney, Saha and Van Nistelrooy. Physically he wasn't ready and he didn't know the game in England at all. At first, he didn't look cut out for it physically. But he got in the gym, bulked up a bit, watched the game and learnt quickly. And over time he became the great player he is. He was always tough, and he worked out how to play in England. Tackles and challenges that we let go in the Premier League would be fouls in Europe and Russia, so he just needed time to get his head around it.

As partners we complemented each other perfectly. But it's hard to explain why. It was an instinctive thing. Defenders need to be able to *smell* danger. He smelled one type of danger, I smelled a different type of danger, and then we'd

ON DEFENDING

just work off each other's instincts. Somehow I always knew exactly what he was going to do, and he knew exactly what I was going to do so we dovetailed. Some relationships on the pitch are easy to explain, and you can go and talk about them and go into detail. But they're the ones that don't flow naturally. My partnership with Vida was very natural, it just kind of happened.

Part of defending is one-to-one duels. The other part is being aware of the shape around you. If you've got 11 players all winning their duels around the pitch, then you've got a chance. But you've got to be set up in the right way to win your duels. So it's a bit of both, really. I used to think: 'As long as I'm beating my two strikers, or the one striker and the number ten behind him, as long as they think I'm too strong and too quick, and too bright and too switched-on for them, we've got a chance of winning.' And that's what me and Vida used to say to each other: 'if we do our job, we keep a clean sheet, we'll win this game.'

Relentless

Win

Win

Win

Just win

Some time after Ben Foster left Manchester United he gave an interview saying he couldn't understand the club or the players. One of the things that seemed to bother him was what happened after we won the Carling Cup against Spurs. Ben was in goal that day, played really well and was named man of the match after we won on penalties. But we barely celebrated and he didn't get to enjoy it as he might have done. You see, our minds immediately switched to the next important match. We had a big league game coming at Newcastle, and then a Champions League second leg against Inter. So, great, we won the cup. We had pictures taken out on the pitch, and then we came in and behaved much like we would after any normal game of football. 'What's next?' The cup was sitting in the corner somewhere and no one took much notice of it. It seems Ben was upset by this. In retrospect it was one of the big, special days of his career but it passed him by a bit.

Looking back, I can understand a little how he felt because now I realise we never did much celebrating of *any* of our triumphs. If you'd asked me at the time, I'd have said Ben should have been thinking, 'I'm going to be here for another five years and I'm going to have loads more moments like this and I'll enjoy them once I've retired.' Now I think: You know what? I wish we'd taken the time to enjoy that a bit more. On the other hand, maybe that attitude of never being too pleased with ourselves was part of the secret of winning. In that case, we didn't just want to win the Carling Cup. We wanted to win the Premier League, the Champions League, everything. That was always the mentality. It's how we trained. Intensity was always really high. It was relentless. We played to win every game and were never satisfied.

A key part of it, I think, was that we never stood back to pat ourselves on the back. A lot of that came from the manager, but it was in the players too.

How many cups and titles and trophies did we win? I lost count. How many victory parades did we have? I can only remember one before we won the league in Fergie's last season. And by then I was able to appreciate it more than at other times because I'd fought back from injury and knew I probably wouldn't have too many more occasions like that. So I relished it. But the previous times, we never really dwelt on our achievement or soaked them up. We'd win the league and immediately think: Right. Onto the next one. Next season, what are we doing? I fancy us next year.

That's not how it is with other clubs. Burnley come second in the Championship and get promoted to Premier League. What do they do? They celebrate with an open-top bus victory parade to the town hall! Arsenal beat Hull City and win the FA Cup – their first trophy in nearly ten years. What do they do? Organise an open-top bus tour! Manchester City win the league – they do an open-top bus tour!

In my 12 years at United it just wasn't something we did. Like winning the league wasn't that big a deal. Yeah, of course we won the league, we usually do, it's normal. 'But shouldn't we have a parade?'

'Nah, we're not doing that again. It costs more than a hundred grand and we're only going to have to do it all again next year.'

That seemed to be the club's attitude. We really didn't enjoy things the way we should have done. But we did keep winning.

I remember when we came back from winning the Champions League in Moscow there were just a couple of hundred people waiting at the airport. We got off the plane, had some pictures taken and then it was basically: 'Cheers, see you later. See you in pre-season.' And that was it! No open-top bus tour! If any other club just won the Premier League and the Champions League they'd at least hire a bus! Most other cities would close down and party for a day or two!

I only really started noticing the difference when other teams started doing it. Chelsea won the league, and I'm thinking, fucking hell, look how good that looks! I was jealous. Manchester City and Chelsea doing an open-top parade ... How the fuck do they think they're entitled to do that? These moments are special, things don't last forever, and we should have done more of that.

But it was part and parcel of the winning state of mind Fergie created at the club. I remember Robin van Persie loving that. He told me that at Arsenal you *wanted* to win, but at United you *had* to win. It was a big difference. And it's something I really loved too when I first arrived. It was great to feed off that United mentality because I'd always had some of that attitude myself but I'd never before been in a team capable of winning consistently. Sometimes people misread my state of mind on the pitch. I've never shown a lot of emotion – until we win. That's when you see me explode with relief and joy and you see me screaming and pumping my fists. It's not so much a feeling of satisfaction. It's more like a feeling of relief ... And then you move onto the next thing.

Growing up, my Mum and Dad ingrained their work ethic into me. Dad worked so hard; he'd work Saturday nights and Sundays and Mum worked all hours looking after other people's kids. But I'm not sure where my idea of always wanting to be the *best* came from. It wasn't just in football: in everything I did I wanted to be the best, and the best I could be. We used to race at school all the time and I'd notice there were people who were quick but would say 'nah, I don't want to race today.' Looking back, I realise they didn't really have a competitive edge; they were never going to be sports people. But if there was a race to be had, even if I thought

I might not win, I'd always want to see if I could improve, get faster, get closer to the front. I used to run in my socks because I thought that was faster and my Mum would see the holes and say, 'What's going on? You're wearing through your socks like there's no tomorrow,' and I was like 'Yeah, Mum, but I'm getting *faster*.' I always had that edge. And I always played football against kids older than me so I had to work harder.

I remember an incident at school when we played in the Metropolitan Police five-a-sides and our goalkeeper was shit. He wasn't actually even our goalkeeper because our real goalkeeper hadn't turned up, and this kid took his place and let in a crucial goal that meant we got beat in one of the group games. And I remember going crazy hammering him. 'What's wrong with you?' I shouted, 'You can't even save a goal, you're *rubbish*, I can't believe it. Next time, put someone else in goal. If you can't do it get out.' He started crying.

I said, 'Why you crying man? You baby, you're a baby, you're a baby.' My Dad had to come over and say, 'Rio, what's wrong with you? Calm down.'

I really enjoyed my time at West Ham and Leeds but I never tasted anything near success. When I came to Manchester United, I just bought immediately into the mentality of winning a game and then moving onto the next one until you get to the final hurdle which is winning the trophy ... and that's when you enjoy it. But the whole process is strictly business: don't take your eye off the ball, don't look too far ahead, don't look back. If you haven't got that element of nastiness, that single-mindedness, that will to win at all costs, if you've not got that, then Manchester United isn't the place for you.

I'm not sure why, but the team that reached its peak in 2008, hasn't quite had the recognition it deserves. In terms of statistics, it's the most successful period the club ever had. Three Champions League finals in four years, back to back League titles, three on the bounce and it should have been four … it's quite a record! I remember a few of the lads talked about it not long ago and the consensus was that we hadn't yet got the credit we deserved for what we achieved over eight or nine years. In time I think people will probably look back and say, 'you know what? That was a hell of a team.'

Actually, I was part of three teams. The first was with Ruud van Nistelrooy, Veron, Beckham, Nicky Butt, Roy Keane, Giggs. Then it evolved and we had a transitional period where we didn't win the League for a couple of years. Then they all left, bar Giggsy and we had a new team with Vidić, Evra, Rooney and Ronaldo, Tevez, and we started winning again. Then you add Carrick, Fletcher, O'Shea. And then there's the last team with Nani, and Danny Welbeck, Tom Cleverley, Ashley Young, Kagawa, Chicarito and then we won the league again with Robin van Persie.

If you put our 2008 team up against any team in the history of Man United, I think we'd win. We'd overrun any of them, and we had magic in Ronaldo the other teams just couldn't stop. The '99 Treble winners were great but they didn't have a game-changer like Ronaldo. Think what we had. Up front: Ronaldo and Rooney with Carlos Tevez backing them up. Not bad, eh? In midfield Carrick, Scholes and Owen Hargreaves, and the incredible running of Ji-Sung Park with Nani to come in when you need him. At the back Gary Neville or Wes Brown at right back, me and Vida in the middle, Patrice Evra left back and the great Edwin van der Sar in goal. I don't care what anyone says. That team ain't getting touched!

I'm too young to have seen the '68 team or anything before that, but I reckon we were stronger than anything the club has had going back to the 80s. Older guys can debate about the great teams of the past but we'd have given anyone problems. And not just the old United teams. I think we'd have been too quick for the great Liverpool teams of the 80s and 70s. We'd have had too much firepower for the best Arsenal sides, though their 2004 'Invincibles' would have been our toughest game, because they were a strong, physical, quick, and intelligent side, and in Thierry Henry they had a guy who could create something from nothing.

And has any English team had a winning mentality quite like ours? I was lucky to join and learn from a group of players who knew what it took to win the league, how to make sure you didn't drop points at places like Bolton and Southampton. Guys like Keane, Beckham, Giggs, Scholes and Gary Neville weren't fazed by anything. They approached vital matches without nerves. They made even the biggest occasions feel like just another game. The approach was always: calm, cool, relaxed, focused, clear-headed. Always prepare the same way. Don't get involved with nerves or extra shouting. Never get carried away by hype or emotion. Never think: 'we've got to win this match to win the league'. Just go out, get your three points, be normal.

The collapse of Liverpool when they should have won the league in 2014 was a perfect example of how not to do it. You can't blame them for getting emotional over the Hillsborough anniversary. It's an emotional club with some of the most emotional fans in the country. I understand that very well because United have the tragedy of Munich and United's fans are incredibly emotional, too. But you saw what happened after the 25th anniversary of the disaster. The Liverpool players seemed to get caught up in the heightened feelings. They started treating each game as something absolutely out of the ordinary, as the be-all and end-all of their careers almost, as the chance to 'make history'... So they stopped playing their normal game and they ended up dropping points they wouldn't normally have dropped. In the famous game against Crystal Palace, when they let in three late goals to draw 3-3, you saw them getting agitated and nervous and losing control of the situation. As soon as Palace scored one goal, Liverpool's positive mentality evaporated and it felt like they were suddenly facing an avalanche. They were looking at each other as if to say, 'what should we do? What happens next?'

You need to know how to win – and how to keep doing it.

Going back to Ben Foster and that League Cup final, he was thinking 'come on, let's just enjoy this a bit', while the rest of us were thinking: let's get onto the next thing, it's just the League Cup, we've got other things to win this year ...

Win. Win. Win. Just win. If you can't buy into that, then,

sorry, you're not going to be there very long. Ben Foster, unfortunately for him, wasn't at Manchester United very long. Some people might see that as nutty but for me it's just a way of life.

Fergie set the tone; we took our cue from him. When we beat Chelsea in Moscow, it didn't feel like we'd achieved what we set out to achieve. Not at all. It wasn't Matt Busby closing a chapter ten years after Munich. It wasn't Bill Shankly going into the Celtic dressing room after they won the European Cup and telling Jock Stein: 'you're immortal now.' Within about an hour of us lifting the trophy, the gaffer was saying: 'Right, next season … let's make sure we're back here next season.' It wasn't: 'OK that's finished.' It was all about winning again. Then winning more. Then some more.

When I was at United we won six league titles, but in my mind it should have been eight or nine. In 2004 we were damaged by my long ban for missing the drug test. When I came out of the team we were three points ahead of Arsenal. If I'd been able to play the whole season, we could've won that year. In 2010 we lost by one point to Chelsea – but Drogba's winning goal at our place a few weeks earlier was offside.

As for losing on goal difference to City in 2012 … how did that happen? At almost the end of the last day of the season, we'd won at Sunderland and City were losing 2–1 to QPR in injury time. It was in the bag. How did QPR *not* hold out in the last couple of minutes? I later found out that their goalkeeping coach Kevin Hitchcock came onto the side of the pitch and was shouting 'We're safe! We're safe!' meaning results had gone their way and they weren't getting relegated. To me, that suggests they downed tools. They wouldn't have been thinking consciously about affecting our game. I just think it's a natural thing after being under so much pressure – they felt relief and relaxed in the last couple of minutes. And that's why what happened happened.

Meanwhile, we were waiting on the pitch at Sunderland. One minute we're thinking 'We've won because they've got to score two goals in the last minute,' I'm shouting on the sidelines, 'What's the score? What's the score?' I'm thinking: there's no way City can score two, we must win now! All of a sudden you hear the Sunderland fans cheering. And you think 'OK, they got one, but surely they can't get another one.' Then the Sunderland fans go again and we're all looking around at each other thinking: 'Are they winding us up?' City can't have scored two goals in a minute. And you can't do anything about it. You just walk off the pitch numb. You think, fuck me, what's gone on here? It was just unbelievable. We'd had a bad time at Sunderland before: the year before, or a couple of years before, sewage pipes broke in our changing room and the ceiling fell in and there was shit all over everyone's clothes ... and then we lose the league up there and their fans are cheering for us losing.

So how did the gaffer react? I remember him in the changing room afterwards: 'You fucking *remember* this! You young boys are going to be here a long time ... you're going to come back here ... remember how this mob up here *cheered* when you lost the league the way you did ...'

Remember it we did. The next year we came back and won the league.

Back Story

You know the moment I realised I had to get treatment?
It was when I played against Liverpool.
Torres was on fire but I'd never had a problem with him.

But now there was a moment in the box.
He put the ball past me,
I turned,
We ran,
We went shoulder to shoulder.
Any other time I woulda won that ball,
Any other time I woulda won that ball all day long.

I remember coming off the pitch.
We lost the game, I think; or we drew.
The manager said to me the next day: 'That's not the real Rio Ferdinand.
Any other day you'd have swept that ball up.
You'd have took it off him before he even thought about shooting.
You can't let that keep happening.

*You've gotta go and get yourself sorted out because you're not ...
you're not fit.'*

*And he was right.
'Cos I was missing training sessions all week,
Then playing the games,
And that was it.
So I'm not fit.
I'm not match fit.
I'm obviously not match fit.*

Until I was 30 I never had any injuries. Fit as a fiddle, I was. Played every game, 45 or 50 a season. In training, I'd just go out and smash balls about, jump straight into it at 100 miles an hour without any stretching or warming up. That was how I'd always been as a kid and I just carried on like that. But I remember Ryan Giggs saying to me: 'Once you hit 30 your body changes. You have to take care of yourself more.'

I thought, 'Yeah, right.' It was like when you're a kid and people say 'Enjoy your school years, they're the best time you'll ever have' and you go 'Yeah, yeah ...' You take it with a pinch of salt. Then I hit 30, and Giggsy was right: it was like someone flicked a switch!

I started picking up little niggles. I was getting these little tears, small tears in my groin and in my hamstrings. I didn't know why. Then we had this game against Stoke. I was fine before; the night before I was perfect. And we're doing our warm-up and I jump. It's just a jump – a normal part of warming-up. But as I land I feel my lower back go. And

BACK STORY

the pain was just ridiculous – crazy pain – the craziest, most unbelievable instability. I was almost bent double.

That was the start of it all.

It became the weirdest thing because I never understood what was wrong with me. Nor did the doctors or the back specialists or the physios. I had some exercises which sometimes helped. But mostly I was taking tablets; I was taking so many painkillers and anti-inflammatories I could have opened my own chemist. When it was really bad I'd be bent over and my back would be arched and I'd walk like an old man.

I didn't sleep a lot of the time. I thought I'd have to retire; I thought I might be damaged for the rest of my life.

I tried everything: I went all over the North West; I went to London; I went to Germany; I was having manipulations from chiropractors. I'd find one chiropractor I thought was really good and I'd use him for three or four months. But I'd still be getting the problems, so I'd search for someone else. I saw Muller Wolfart, a renowned specialist with Bayern Munich and the German national team. He had his own private practice in Munich and I went there quite regularly for a few months. He'd give me injections and I'd be sorted – but only short term. For big games, he'd get me right quickly. Like if we had a league decider on the Saturday, then a quarter final of the Champions League or a semi-final … that sort of thing.

Then I got back in touch with a guy called Kevin Lidlow in London who helped me when I thought I'd need surgery on my knee. He gave me exercises for the injury and I didn't have to have the operation, so I knew he was good. Kevin was great at manipulations and stuff like that, and he used to get me back into good nick in a couple of hours. *Almost* good nick, anyway. He looked after a lot of the England rugby team and is well thought of.

But even he could only get me to a certain point. Nothing would work long term.

So I developed a weekly routine. I'd play on the Saturday and then I'd be debilitated from the moment I got home after a game. I couldn't walk properly at all on the Sunday and I wouldn't even attempt to train. I'd just do warm down stuff, like going in the pool, trying to get my posture back. Then, if I took some tablets, if we had a game on the Wednesday, I might be able to play. Or if I didn't take tablets, and we had a game on the Saturday, then I'd wait. By Thursday I might be able to do some jogging. By Friday I'd train with the team. Then I'd play again.

The same cycle would repeat itself. It went on like for 18 months! The doctors worked out it was a problem in my lower back – the SI joint, L3 and L4 – and they couldn't fix it. Between 2009 and 2010 – that was the worst time.

I couldn't even go in the garden with my kids. That used to kill me. My boy would say. 'Dad, can you come in the garden and play football?'

'Oh, lads I can't. I can't get out there at the moment.'

I felt awful. I couldn't even stand up for longer than a couple of minutes. I just about managed to get out for the school run, then get back to the car and have to take a deep breath. At night I'd wake up, sweating, thinking 'Fuck me;

BACK STORY

I'm going to have to retire. I don't want to go out like this. I don't want to go out on a sick-note.'

Some days bed was the only place my back felt comfortable. I'd get up and try to move around in the afternoon. Then, when the kids went to bed, I'd just lie down and watch TV. Most days I'd basically lie down and watch the sports channel, or reality TV.

There was so much fear and anxiety about being injured. At times I almost wished I had something straightforward like a broken leg. With some injuries you *know*: if you get a cruciate it's six months; a broken leg it's a couple of months. Meniscus is four weeks. You know how long so you've got the light at the end of the tunnel. Not having that light ate away at me. Bad back? No one knew what was wrong. Not the top specialist, not even the top physios. I thought: 'If they don't know, who else will? How am I ever going to get better?'

It must seem strange to an outsider. But you have to remember football is still a 'macho man' culture. I'd never been injured before, so I'd never had those thoughts going through my head. Looking back I think I was projecting my feelings onto other people. I would have looked at myself and thought 'Fucking hell, I reckon he can play, he just don't fancy it this week. We've got Everton this week and big Duncan Ferguson's playing so he just don't fancy it ...' At West Ham I used to think Paolo di Canio wouldn't play in certain games. He'd play at home and be a macho man, but I'd think 'He won't turn up next week 'cos it's Everton away.'

Sometimes I was right. Sometimes I was wrong. But that was my mentality: you should be out there no matter what.

Looking back I can see the whole psychology was weird. I should have been more balanced. Injuries are part of football – everyone knows that. But I felt ashamed; I'd walk into the training ground like a *mouse*, hugging the walls and doors. I didn't want anyone to see me; I didn't want to have contact with anyone. To be honest, I didn't want to go to the training ground at all. I tried to arrive when the lads had gone out for training so no one would see me. You're embarrassed. You think: 'The lads are all having a banter and I'm not out there.' You don't feel part of it. You feel lonely. You feel insecure.

Do the lads think I'm shirking?

Do they think I don't want to play anymore?

Do they think I'll never get back to what I was?

So you don't want to be around them. I'd always been one of the bigger personalities in the changing room: bubbly, up for a laugh. But you become subdued. Even around the physios and sports scientists and coaches. When I wasn't playing they'd see me around the training ground, and they'd be a bit subdued and I'd be a bit subdued. But as soon as I got back to training, the difference was obvious first time out on the pitch. Suddenly they were loud and lively again: 'Oh, I can tell you're back, fucking hell!' The difference was just immediate. When I went back into training, the lads would be laughing at me. I'd walk in and they'd take the piss and say: 'Oh fuck, look at him!' or 'Rio's alright. Rio can train today.'

I didn't really let on to the doc, or the gaffer or anyone how much pain I was probably in 'cos I just wanted to keep playing. I thought 'If I don't play, the manager's going to go and try and buy someone else.' That didn't help me in the long run. I thought I'd find the cure.

The lads weren't much help. But to be honest I'm the same. When you've got an injury you don't want to burden anyone else with it and you try and get back as quick as possible. When you're playing, there's so much going on, you're so busy being worried about getting yourself ready for the game – physically, mentally – you're a little bit selfish. I remember when Louis Saha was at United. He had a lot of injuries, and when I look back, he must have been feeling really shit. You'd see him every day and I remember saying to him 'What you doing, man? How's the injury? When you back?' And he'd go 'Oh I don't know, man' and slope off. When I look back I realise he must have been thinking 'I don't even want to *see* Rio because all he ever fucking does is ask me about my fucking injury.' You think you're being concerned and showing an interest, but he's probably got every member of the squad saying that. Sometimes you just have to leave people to it.

There's an old-school idea in English football that you have to play on whatever. A lot of foreign players, if they get injuries, that's it: they shut down and down tools. We say: 'Look at them, the flipping pansies, they just play one game, it's a big game we need them to play and he's not even going to hurt himself just a little bit to play.' But invariably these guys go on for a bit longer than us because they take themselves out of the firing line when they get a little niggle and don't let themselves get exposed to more injuries.

We're a bit more stupid; we think we're 'Braveheart'. It's your personal pride. The gaffer says 'Are you ready to play or not?' When I can't actually walk, I've had to say: 'Sorry, boss, I just can't.' But you sit there doubting yourself; you think, 'Did I really say that?' You know deep down you can't play but you're still thinking: 'But could I? Could I go out there and play? Oh no! I've let the manager down!'

You're always playing with your own mind. 'Am I cheating him? Am I cheating myself? Am I cheating the club?' Really and truly, if you did play you'd be probably letting the club down and you might be out for longer which will let the club down even further.

Strangely enough, Alex Ferguson was really easy with injuries. He had such a big squad that you being injured sometimes worked in his favour. If someone got injured he could give someone else a game. Unless it was a really massive game and he thought: 'I need him to play.' Then he'd show his disappointment. But he'd never push you to play. He'd say 'Just let me know. Let me know on Friday… or let me know in the morning.' That way he could make his decision on what to do.

I was trying to mask the extent of the problem from everybody. Probably the club doctor had an idea. But the amount of tablets I was taking … I wouldn't tell anyone how bad it really was. If I had my time again I would have just stopped and said 'I need to find a way to solve this.' But I didn't see a way out. I thought: 'I've got to either keep playing like this or retire because this is just too much, and I'm not going to be able to walk when I finish football.' It was crazy.

BACK STORY

I had some really depressive moments. You think: am I ever going to play properly again? At top level? Are my kids ever going to be able to watch me play? What the hell's going on? You don't ask yourself once every few months or once a week – it's continuous. When you're driving into the training ground it's 'How many more times will I be doing this?'

Compounding the problem, you've got people in the media saying: 'Oh he's gone. His legs have gone ... He's injury prone.' People in the street stop you and ask 'When you coming back? Are you all right or what? What's going on?' You don't even want to talk to anyone! Every person walking by is asking you about your injury! Actually I used that later. People doubting me, writing me off; that was my fuel, my fuel to work that extra bit harder to come back.

The other thing that really bothered me is ... I can't imagine my life without playing football. I can't imagine giving my place up in the team or letting someone else have an opportunity to prove themselves. I was so scared of not being able to get back in the team – of not playing. I was scared of having to give up doing what I do every day and what I *love*.

Yet loads of people, hundreds of people ... all they can talk about is money! People came up to me and said 'Oh, it don't matter 'cos you're earning loads of money.' It's what people write on social media: 'Don't worry. What do you care? You're earning hundreds of grands a week or whatever.' People think that money is the route to all happiness and that it solves all the problems. But there's more to life than earning money. OK it's easy for me to say – I know – but once you get past a certain point with money, the only thing you're thinking about is what you love. To be stopped from doing something you love, no matter how much money you've got … it's hard to deal with that.

As it happens, I was thinking about money in a completely different way. I was thinking: if I'm injured, should they even be paying me? I really worried about it. Do I warrant getting paid this money?

I remember my Dad saying to me 'Look what you've done for the club.' And friends said: 'Of course you deserve it. You've helped win things. You've been a part of winning teams. You've not missed a lot of games through injury before. You've not cheated anyone. The club knows that. Anyway, it's part of the game, being injured, and the club understands that.'

But I couldn't get on board with that; I was embarrassed. I'd think to myself: the manager must be sitting there thinking 'Fucking hell, we are paying him all this money and look at him, sitting on his arse.' Then I'd see the chief executive David Gill, and think: 'He must be thinking the same thing.' And I'd think the fans must be thinking the same thing. Going round and round in my head were the thoughts I thought people must be thinking about me. Even though they quite possibly didn't think any of those things.

And eventually … well, I got lucky.

Just when I was getting really depressed, and thinking it was all over, the doctor at the club, Dr McAnally, found a clinic in Milton Keynes called the Blackberry Clinic. They specialise in doing scans so they can see how your back looks when it moves. There's an injection they give you into a small area where the pain is and they use the scan to watch how your back moves under stress. They found that certain ligaments in my lower back were very weak and that was the reason for all these problems – the groin and hamstring and calf problems too. I'd been compensating for the back weakness by making all the forces going through my body go to the wrong place.

The cure was surprisingly simple: injections. They injected a sugar formula to stiffen the ligaments. No cortisone, no drugs; just a sugar to strengthen the ligaments that attach the bones together in my spine. It was almost like an immediate 'Eureka!' moment. My back suddenly felt secure again: I didn't feel the instability; I didn't feel like my back was about to break. So I had a course of injections – six injections over six weeks. The pain was unbelievable. But you know me! Being the man I am, I coped – no problem!

Actually it hurt like hell. But afterwards I was up and running, and it was the most fantastic feeling. I now appreciate things I used to take for granted – like being properly fit, playing at the highest level, and competing for titles and trophies. In 2010 I played a load of games, and the season after that I made the most appearances by any of our defenders – and we won the league. I still need painkillers occasionally and twice a year I have to have top-up injections. But the nightmare was over almost as suddenly as it began. I came back; I proved I could still play at the highest level; I proved the doubters wrong.

I felt great again.

On Racism

My Mum's white
My Dad's black
I see things from a white perspective
And a black perspective
Just respect each other
That's all I want for my kids
I don't think it's a hard thing to ask for

1. LULLED

My Mum and Dad's story would make a film. They'd be walking together and passers-by would spit on Mum because she was walking with a black guy. Other times they'd be stopped by the police. Dad would be treated badly by the police and others on the estate. *For being with a white woman.* And Mum would get treated badly too. By the police. *For being with a black guy.*

It sounds like a story from apartheid South Africa, doesn't it? But that was London in the 1970s. That's the kind of shit my parents had to go through to have my brothers and me.

Now I'm a Dad and my wife is white. And I don't want our kids to have to go through the same crap.

When I was growing up in Peckham there was plenty of racism around but you never knew when you'd run into it, or how toxic it would be, or exactly how to react. My estate was a real mixture of people: Irish, English, African, Caribbean, Turkish. Mostly we all got on well and played together. But there was also an older set of guys we'd play with every now and again who were all white. They were mostly Millwall or Arsenal fans and you'd definitely hear racist comments from them sometimes. One time we were playing and these guys started making monkey noises at us. *Ubu babba, Ubu babba …* that kind of thing. We were much younger and smaller than them, so it really wasn't a fight we could physically fight. But we had something in common as well. Football. They were good at football, and so were we. So we'd play against them. Or, to put it another way, we'd play *with* them. Football was a bringer-together. Football trumped everything else. We might not like these guys sometimes but we'd play together for hours at a time. And while we were playing we'd be knitted together. But you'd hear the odd racist comment, especially if we were winning. So then the question became: what are we going to do about this? Well, all we really could do was say, 'fuck off.' It wouldn't go further. In my mind, I always had the ultimate back-up. If things got proper serious, I could've told my Dad and he'd have sorted them all out. But I never did, because I wanted to keep playing football against better players, with these guys. So we kept it in the background and never spoke about it.

ON RACISM

Of course it was different if anyone off the estate ever said anything like that. That was a fight straight away. Looking back, it seemed a weird way to deal with that situation. But when I was younger my first reaction when someone said something racist was always to fight. When I got older, I'd exact revenge in a different way. I'd think: right, I have to win this game now. Or I've got to score. I remember going for my first training session at Charlton. One of their kids called me a 'black bastard' and we got into a fight immediately. The response of their coach John Cartwright was brilliant. He stepped in, took my side, made the boy apologise and banned him for a few weeks. I hadn't even signed for Charlton. I was impressed.

On the estate Mum was magnificent. My next door neighbour called me a 'black bastard' and when I knocked on the door for her daughter to come out and play, I heard her say, 'don't let that nigger in the door.' I went back to Mum and said, 'what's a nigger?' I didn't know. I was only young. Mum went straight round, kicked the door down and dragged the woman out and made her apologise to me.

Much later, I became aware of racism in professional football. I'd seen that picture of my hero John Barnes contemptuously back-heeling a banana some racist had thrown at him on the pitch. I knew players like Paul Ince, Brendon Batson and Viv Anderson were getting grief. I'd seen stadium racism first-hand too, when I went with a mate to see Millwall play Derby. Derby had four or five black players and they were all playing well. This geezer in front of us was going, 'those fucking black bastards, send them back to where they're fucking from.' Then he turned around and noticed me. There was a policeman standing right next to me. I looked at the policeman and he looked through me like nothing had been said. Then the guy says: 'not you, mate, just the ones on the pitch.' I just got up and said to my friend: 'I'm leaving, man. I can't deal with this shit.'

I never heard anything like that at West Ham. There never seemed to be a problem with being black and playing for West Ham. In the 1970s they had Clyde Best and Ade Coker. Paul Ince had come through there, so had George Parris. West Ham always had a few black players. I felt very comfortable at the club. And by the late 1990s and 2000s things seemed to have improved all over the country. You weren't hearing racist comments at grounds in England any more. If incidents happened abroad with the national team or the Under 21s, as happened in Spain and Serbia and other places, the FA responded strongly. The media seemed okay on the subject, too. I thought our game, and our FA, were doing well and should be applauded. Organisations like Show Racism The Red Card and Kick It Out seemed to be doing a good job too, and I did events for them. I remember doing a campaign with Thierry Henry and telling people: 'I'm not seeing racism in the stands,' and 'England has done a great job.'

Then, on 15th October 2011, Manchester United played Liverpool at Anfield. In the sixty-second minute, as Patrice Evra marked Luis Suárez at a corner, they started speaking to each other in Spanish. I was a couple of yards away and didn't hear a thing. To quote from the later FA report, the conversation went like this:

Patrice Evra: Fucking hell, why did you kick me?
Luis Suarez: Because you're black.
Patrice Evra: Say it to me again, I'm going to kick you.
Luis Suarez: I don't speak to blacks.
Patrice Evra: OK, now I think I'm going to punch you.
Luis Suarez: OK, blackie, blackie, blackie.

It was a Frenchman and a Uruguayan talking in Spanish but the conversation and its aftermath was big news in England for months. After much strife, Suarez was found guilty by the FA of racial abuse, and was fined and banned for eight games. At the two clubs, football tribalism kicked in immediately. At Manchester United we backed Pat, of course. We knew him as a serious, genuine guy who'd made a serious allegation. He'd never lied about anything before, why would he lie now? By contrast Liverpool players and their manager instinctively backed their man, saying Suarez was a great guy. The way Liverpool circled the wagons and later all wore Suarez T-shirts ... it left a bad taste. They wanted to show solidarity to their teammate, but they were missing the bigger picture. They got right and wrong mixed up.

What worried me more in those first few days was the reaction further afield. I was shocked by how much sympathy there was for Suarez. Huge numbers of people in the media and social media were saying: 'Poor Suarez, maybe there's nothing racist about it. Maybe in Uruguay this is inoffensive.

Poor lad, he's culturally confused, and he's getting punished for nothing.' Nobody even talked about the pressure on Pat. How could it get turned around so that racism was being defended and drawing attention to racism was being attacked? How could that happen in our game in this day and age? I didn't understand it. People paid lip service to the idea that racism was *a bad thing*. But they obviously didn't have a clue what racism actually was, or how its victims felt. It was a real shock to discover racism had never actually gone away – it was just much better hidden than before. We'd been lulled into a false sense of security. It had been swept under the carpet all these years. Just one little paper-cut of an incident made it clear it was all still there, just below the surface.

I'd only been a few feet from that conversation between Patrice and Suarez. It never occurred to me that racism was just about to come a whole lot closer.

2. ANTON

Six days after the Evra–Suarez incident I was sitting at home watching on TV as QPR played Chelsea in a league match. QPR were winning 1–0, and my brother Anton was having a great game in the QPR defence. About five minutes from the end, Anton and John Terry had an argument in the QPR penalty area. We then saw John jogging back into his own half before the television director cut to a close-up. You didn't need to be a professional lip-reader to see that John Terry, captain of England, my defensive partner in the national team for the last six years, had just said: 'you fucking black cunt.' And he seemed to have said it in Anton's direction. In less than a minute my phone began to go crazy. My mates, my family, practically everybody I knew were texting and calling to say: 'Did you *see* that?' Within minutes Twitter was going nuts and the clip was on YouTube.

The consequences of that moment were confused, disastrously drawn-out and are still felt. The matter could and should have been sorted out cleanly and quickly in a way that would have allowed everyone – including John Terry – to emerge with dignity. Instead, it festered horribly for nearly a year and caused great harm.

For those who didn't follow the formal proceedings case, these were the main points. The police, acting on an anonymous complaint from a member of the public, eventually charged John Terry with racially abusing Anton. John Terry denied the charges and at various times offered different explanations. After a five-day trial, in July 2012 – 9 months after the incident – he was acquitted. The magistrate found that John Terry had indeed said 'you fucking black cunt' but couldn't say if he had done so with racist intent. Two months later, in September 2012, an FA disciplinary committee took a different approach. It found him guilty of 'using abusive and/or insulting words and/or behaviour' and imposed a four-match ban and a £220,000 fine.

At this point, John was still maintaining his innocence. But two weeks later, he issued an apology of sorts 'to everyone,' saying that while he was 'disappointed' by the FA's decision 'with the benefit of hindsight my language was clearly not an appropriate reaction to the situation for someone in my position.' But he never apologised to me or to Anton. And he has never hinted that he has ever had a moment of understanding over the damage his stupidity had inflicted on everyone. Meanwhile, amid all the uncertainty and bad feeling, my England career had been wrecked while John's lurched on in a confused fashion until it, too, hit the buffers. At first, he carried on playing. Then he was stripped of the England captaincy. Then he played. Then he retired. As I'll explain later, this too could have been avoided.

While the case was going on Anton's lawyers told us we couldn't speak about it publicly – and we didn't. This I now feel was a mistake. If we had spoken out some of the distress and pain might have been avoided. The case damaged football and race relations in Britain. Anton, the innocent party in all this, had his career damaged and was subjected to death threats, bullets in the post, and unending racist abuse. My mum had her windows smashed and bullets put through her door, and ended up in hospital with a virus because of the stress. I felt that the legal and football authorities made mistakes all the way through. The criminal prosecution was misguided and FA dithering made things worse. Indeed, few people covered themselves in glory. Some of the elder statesmen among black British footballers were conspicuous by their absence in terms of speaking out publicly. We disagreed with people who wanted to use the case to advance a political agenda, and we weren't impressed when Kick It Out paid lip service to the idea of taking a strong stand and then went missing when it counted.

ON RACISM

The FA was confused and indecisive. Caught between wanting to protect the England captain and realising they would have to punish him, they ended up sending mixed messages. Chelsea, who seemed to have no thought beyond wanting to keep their captain in action, added fuel to the fire. Ashley Cole, who'd been a good friend of mine and had known Anton since he was a kid, betrayed that friendship. The biggest idiot of all was John Terry who could have saved everyone a lot of pain by admitting immediately that he had used the words in the heat of the moment but was no racist. I think that's probably what happened and what the truth is. We would have accepted that but he never gave us the chance.

There's one point I'd like to stress. People think Anton took John Terry to court. That's completely wrong. Anton actually urged the police and the Crown Prosection Service (CPS) *not* to prosecute. He knew a court case would generate more heat than light, create antagonism and make people take sides. But neither he nor I ever had a say in the matter. What happened was that a member of the public made an anonymous complaint, the police investigated and then the CPS decided to prosecute. Then the trial was delayed so John could play at Euro 2012.

Anton always made it clear he hadn't heard the words on the pitch. It was John Terry's lawyers who summoned Anton to court, not the other way round. That's what people need to understand. I can't stress it enough: Anton was not the instigator of any of this. He *never heard* the offending words and did nothing to justify the hostile treatment he received from the FA and John Terry's lawyers. Their cross-examination of him in court almost amounted to character assassination. Many people, especially Chelsea fans, seem to think that Anton 'grassed' on John Terry. Anton didn't 'grass' on anyone!

3. WHO YOUR FRIENDS ARE

I no longer talk to Ashley Cole or John Terry. With Ashley it all ended the day he decided to go to court. He didn't even warn us: we had to hear from the lawyers. Anton rang me and my head nearly blew off. 'What do you mean Ashley's going to court? Is he going to speak or you?'

'For John.'

'*What?* Are you winding me up?'

Unfortunately, it was no wind-up.

Looking back, I know Ashley was under pressure. I've thought long and hard about this and wondered how Ashley could have played it differently. What he should have said to John was: 'please keep me out of this because it's going to ruin my relationship with Rio if I go with you, or ruin my relationship with you if I go against you, and I don't want either of those things.' At that point, as a man, John Terry could have said: 'I respect that – thanks,' or 'But Ash, I've not fucking done *anything*! Please can you come on my side and speak to them?' At that point Ashley could have come to me and said: 'Ri, he ain't said it, man,' and I'd have believed him. Just have the conversation like a man! We've known each other since we were kids! He should have come to me as my

ON RACISM

friend and explained that he was in an awkward position. But he never did any of those things.

Instead I had to call – and he still didn't understand. In fact, he reckoned I was out of order for contacting him. I said, 'Ash, what are you doing? My little brother's going through hell, there's bullets through my Mum's letter box, windows getting banged in, and you think *I'm* out of order for ringing you? What world are you living in?' I tried to get him to see it from my perspective. 'What if *your* brother was going to court, and getting hammered in the media, and his career was on the line? Don't you think *you* would be upset with *me* if I was going to court against you? I'd expect you to call me.' But he just didn't get it. Or he did get it but wasn't strong enough to take himself out of the equation. He kept saying: 'I don't want to be a part of this.'

I said: 'Well, you are part of it, you've made yourself a part of it.'

The FA panel eventually decided Ashley's evidence 'evolved' over time to help John's case. That was a polite way of putting it. Ashley refused to give me a coherent explanation; he never gave me a definitive yes or no. All he kept saying was 'but I don't want to be a part of it. I don't want to be here. I don't know what happened, I don't want to be here. I don't want to go to court.' I was like, 'well in that case *why the fuck are you going to court?*'

Our final communication was by text. Just before the trial started at Westminster Magistrates Court, I sent him a message telling him he had a choice: 'You're my mate and you're John Terry's mate. You know both our families. So either go into court and tell the *exact* truth of what happened, or don't go in there at all. You have to make a choice.'

'I've not got a choice,' he said. 'I've been told I've got to go.'

I said, 'well, if you do go just know this: we will never talk again. You know what happened. You saw it with your own eyes. It's not rocket science. I know you never wanted to be involved. Just make your decision.'

'You think I want to come off my holidays to come to court and go through this shit?' was his reply. 'To be involved in it when I don't have to? But that's what I've been told to do.'

I said, 'alright, then. Go. Do it.' And that was it.

I was furious and so disappointed with him. That's what I was feeling when I re-tweeted a comment somebody made on Twitter about Ashley being a 'choc ice': black on the outside, white on the inside. I look back now and think maybe I shouldn't have done it, but it's what I thought and felt at the time. That's the problem with social media: if you're impulsive, you can't turn back the clock. The sad thing is that Ash had always been a good guy and I'd always got on really well with him – he's a nice geezer. We'd been on holiday together; I was at his stag do. We'd both had our problems in the media over the years and found each other's shoulder to lean on. But this one moment has ruined that relationship because I simply could not see my brother go through shit and have one of my so-called mates going to court against him.

I think one day Ashley will understand it properly and feel

ON RACISM

bad. He'll realise his mistake. And we've all made mistakes. I certainly have. There are things I look back and I think I could have been more decent in that situation. So Ashley will get to a certain point in his life, and realise he should at least have rung me to tell me he was going to court. I would have respected that a lot more. If he'd said: 'This is how it is, I've got no choice,' I'd have said 'well, you're a fucking idiot, but at least you've rung me and told me.' He'll look back and be gutted; he'll regret the way he handled it. I can see it was difficult for him and I think the person or people who put him in that position are as much to blame.

As to my relationship with John, there has been a lot of misunderstanding about that as well.

He, too, could have come to me or to Anton. If John had said: 'I think I made a mistake, can we sort this out?' we would have been the first to say: 'you know what? You've been an idiot, but we all make mistakes. I'm not perfect myself. Just don't let it happen again, man.' John would've made a public apology or whatever and the case would have been quickly forgotten. The problem was that he tried to run away from what he'd done. I can't forgive the way he allowed that to ruin friendships: his friendship with myself, my friendship with Ashley ... all gone to waste.

I've never actually spoken to John about the case. What was the point? I'd seen what he'd done. We'd been teammates with England for years. And we could have been again. We weren't close but we'd had nights out, texted or spoken on the phone every now and then. I thought there was always an edge to him, but we got on OK. John certainly never showed himself to me to be racist. I take people at face value. I'll always assume that people are alright until proved otherwise. I never had anything bad to say about John. Of course, there was a club rivalry, but we got on fine on the pitch. Then this happened. But I'm still not convinced he is a racist or was even *being* racist.

John obviously handled the situation badly. He should have just rung my brother and said, 'I'm sorry, man. I said it. But I ain't a racist. If I could take it back I would.' I'd have thought: you know what? He's a fucking stand-up guy. I'll shake his hand. I'd have told him: 'I think you're a prick for saying it, but you've actually come and manned up.' I'd have said, 'yeah, alright.' And I'd probably have got hammered for it. Some people would have said I was a sell-out for even shaking his hand and accepting his apology. And I wouldn't have cared. But John was never man enough to say any of those things.

The whole thing has made me look at Martin Luther King and Nelson Mandela with even more admiration than before. Mandela is one of my heroes because of the way he forgave people. One of the highlights of the trip to South Africa in 2010 was meeting him just before the World Cup. The whole team went, and I remember John being as impressed by the great man as any of us. One of the things I always think is: this business was *nothing* compared to what Nelson Mandela went through in South Africa. He was treated like shit for decades. He went to prison for 27 years. And yet he found the strength to forgive the people who did that to him. How did he do that? Because I find it impossible to forgive or

ON RACISM

forget the pain John put my family through. That was the heart of the matter. Whatever he had or hadn't said became almost a sideshow. I sat there thinking: he was my mate, my teammate, we played 30 or 40 games for England together. We'd competed against each other for years. We weren't best mates but we were football buddies. And he just sat there and watched as my brother went through all this because of his stupidity. That was the betrayal.

I would still have been happy to play for England with him. But that possibility got lost in the grey areas of my relationship with the FA. We've had good and bad times over the years, the FA and I. They banned me for eight months over missing a drugs test in 2003; they fined me £60,000 for my 'choc-ice' tweet. But they eventually did the right thing by banning John for four matches. Personally, after everything that happened, I thought he should've got the same punishment as Suarez. But at least the FA showed they weren't happy with what happened. In fact, giving Terry a ban at all was quite a strong and bold considering he hadn't been convicted in the court case.

But then it got confusing again because the FA let him play for England. What message did that send? What I didn't like was that people then automatically assumed that if he played for England, then I couldn't play for England. They seemed to think we couldn't be on the same pitch together. But it wouldn't have been a problem for me. I've played with people I didn't like for years. There were people at Manchester United I wouldn't go for a drink with, would never call or text. But I played with them. You're professional about it. If

59

a person can help me win, I'll play with him no problem. It's not like we have to go for dinner together. I would probably have gone to see John and said: 'Listen, we're never going to be mates again, but let's just work together to make England a better team.' We would have had a working relationship, and it would have been fine. But no one ever asked.

I found that pretty extraordinary because I'd let it be known. People around the club would ask: 'Would you play with him?' and I'd say: 'Yeah. I ain't got a problem.' I wanted to win and play for England. Hodgson should at least have asked: 'Could you play with John Terry?' If I said 'No,' then, OK, they've established that Rio is out of the equation – or John Terry is out of the equation. Then they can pick one of us. But that conversation never took place!

I just think it could all have been handled much better. But I never showed my hand over it because I don't want people to see I'm feeling bad. People think I'm happy-go-lucky. If people asked how I was feeling I would go: 'I'm alright, man. I'm cool.' Then they'd go: 'but don't you think John Terry is a better player than you?' That shit hurt. I want to play for my country and I should have had 100 caps. Then, eventually, when I sorted out my back problems, and I was playing *really* well, a clamour started for me to be back in the England squad. At that point, at the very last minute, just before Euro 2012 Roy Hodgson comes and says he wants me be in the squad!

That was another case of bad communication – and bad timing. I'd had an injury that almost finished my career but had managed to sort it out with a regular course of injections.

ON RACISM

I then had to schedule those injections and, since I was no longer being picked for England, I'd chosen the international break. Just before one of those, all of a sudden, Roy Hodgson asked me to come back to the England squad. At that moment I had to say no because of my treatment. People said I rejected England but that wasn't the case at all.

One thing the case did clarify was who we could rely on. At the height of the nastiness, people were criticising us, saying, 'it's only a comment, let it go.' I'd say: 'You let it go! I can't let it go because it's too important to let go.'

When my Mum fell ill I was in Manchester most of the time. I couldn't even sit with her at the hospital for long, just days here and there, sometimes only a few hours. And my Dad ... well, the entire time I know he wanted to explode. He had to watch his son almost wasting away and being vilified in the media and he couldn't defend him.

In the middle of all this, Sir Alex Ferguson was brilliant. He sent Mum flowers and spoke to her on the phone. That's the touch he's got. No one else in the game that I've met has it. He'd ring her regularly, just to say, 'Are you OK?' It was his personal touch, from the heart. And my Mum would call me and tell me about it, and be so moved. It really gave her a boost. Fergie probably didn't even know how much that meant.

Mum and Dad showed solidarity together going to court with Anton every day. And Jamie Moralee, who's Anton's agent as well as mine, went to court every day. That was impressive: a white guy going in, day in day out, on a race case on behalf of a black guy. That's putting yourself in the firing line. Jamie has a family: what if some racist pig comes and knocks on his door? That's the type of shit you've got to acknowledge. That took guts and Jamie has guts.

I wish I could say the same for some of the people we expected more from. At the time of the trial, rather late in the day, Kick It Out came to Mum and said, 'What can we do? We're here to provide support.'

'Support? Great,' said my Mum. 'You can walk into that court room with us.'

And they said 'Oh, we'll send someone as an observer.'

'No that's not what we need,' said my Mum. 'Don't send some suit no one knows and no one sees. Send your people in T-shirts to walk in with us. Stand with us so people know this a racism case and you're here on our side.'

'Oh no, we can't do that,' came the reply. They refused.

So Mum said: 'In that case, get out of my house, and don't fucking come near us again.' In the event, they did send a guy called Danny Lynch to the trial – in a suit – and no-one in the press reported his presence. I think Mum was right.

With Kick It Out I felt it was pure lip service. They were useless. So were other organisations. Outside the court, I saw Clark Carlisle of the PFA doing interviews. I said: 'Come in the courtroom.'

'Oh I can't be seen to be going in there.'

'What do you mean? You should be going in there supporting John *and* my brother.' I didn't say 'come and support my brother.' I said this a racism case so come in and

ON RACISM

support three of your players who are members, who put money into your organisation every year.

'Oh, we can't ... We can't get involved like that.' Why not? You're standing out here doing interviews for your documentary! What the fuck's that about? When shit gets real, what happens? Where are you? Where are these people?

Months later, a year after the original incident, 3 months after the court case, after all the horrible things we'd had to go through, Kick it Out organised their T-shirt weekend. They wanted everyone to wear a T-shirt saying 'One Game, One Community.' As if everything was fine now. Problem solved. They asked me if I was going to wear the T-shirt. 'Are you crazy? Not a chance!' If they weren't willing to go into the court room with us, then I wasn't willing to go through the charade of wearing their T-shirt. I know it was tit-for-tat but if I'd worn that T-shirt, my Dad wouldn't have spoken to me. Mum probably would have spoken to me, but she would have been deeply disappointed. And I'd disappointed my Mum and Dad too many times in my life to do it this time.

Then it became a thing in the media. They were talking about me. 'Rio's going to wear the T-shirt!'... 'Rio's NOT going to wear the T-shirt!' I heard lots of players say, 'I ain't wearing that fucking T-shirt. No way!' Then they went out and wore them! When push comes to shove, you find out who your mates are. It changed my opinion a little bit about some people who disappeared under rocks. But I didn't let it affect my relationships and I certainly wouldn't want to *out* them for it. I mean, I didn't ask anyone to boycott the T-shirt. Just don't tell me you're not going to wear it, then wear it. Lip service, again. At the same time, some people were as good as their word. Jason Roberts didn't wear one; Joleon Lescott didn't wear one. I heard the entire Wigan and Swansea squads didn't wear any either.

But inevitably there was a focus on me. The manager had announced in a press conference the day before the game against Stoke: 'all my players will wear it.' I couldn't understand that. I thought, he never asked me. Next day, as we were going out for the warm-up, the kit man, Albert Morgan, comes to me with a T-shirt and gives it to me. I was upset straight away. I said, 'fuck off, Albert.' We had that relationship. I could swear at him and he could swear at me, and the next day it'd be forgotten.

'*Fuck off, Albert!*'

'No, the manager wants you to wear it.'

'I ain't fucking wearing it.'

'No, the manager *wants* you to put it on. You've got to put it on.'

'Listen, Albert: FUCK. OFF.'

So I went out onto the pitch not wearing it. I came back in from the warm-up... and the gaffer fucking exploded.

'*Who do you fucking think you are?* Not wearing that fucking shirt? I've told everyone yesterday you're wearing it! You're fucking meant to wear it. Fucking going out on your own and doing your own thing – who do you think you are?' Blah, blah...

I said, 'you didn't ask me. I was *never* going to wear that fucking T-shirt. I didn't tell you to go on TV and fucking speak about it.'

ON RACISM

'That's it,' came the reply. 'You're fined a week's wages.'
'Well, I'll see you tomorrow.'
'Yeah, you fucking will see me tomorrow, you're fined.'
And that was it. I went out and played and we won the game.

The next day, I had to go and see him in his office and I walked in expecting both barrels. I went in with my hard hat on. He sat down. I didn't even sit down. He said, 'listen, I don't agree with what you've done. I know it's your family and everything, but I just don't agree with you not wearing the T-shirt. You've got to support campaigns like this and organisations like that... I'm a union man.'

'Yeah, but, boss, you never spoke to me about it. You never understood my situation. You don't know what's going on and why I didn't wear it.' I tried to explain that I didn't wear it because Kick It Out hadn't gone to the court case, and I didn't believe in what they do. 'If you didn't believe in an organisation, you'd never put their badge on, would you? If something happened and they didn't do what you expected of them, you would never, *ever* back that organisation, I *know* you wouldn't, boss!'

Then he amazed me. He said, 'listen, I spoke to my wife last night and she said to me, um ... she asked me, "did you ask the boy about it?" And I said no. And she said, "There's your mistake there."' He told me that!

Then he said, 'I don't often admit mistakes. But I understand a little bit why you didn't wear it now. I'm not going to fine you. I should have spoken to you. That's my mistake and

I accept that. I still believe you should have worn the T-shirt. But I respect that you didn't.'

And that was it. I was so impressed. My respect for him just went up even more. I think maybe he respected me a little bit more, because I had a belief and I'd stuck to it, even when there was so much pressure on it. It's a question of solidarity. He was seeing it from a team perspective: 'we do everything together, why are you going out on your own?' I understand that because he wants to win and he wants to show that we're united as a squad. But he hadn't asked me how I felt.

But then Fergie's a man of principle and substance, and there aren't too many like that. One thing I can't bear is the people in positions of influence who just pay lip service, like FIFA with their 'RESPECT' and stupid fines. I just don't believe they're sincere. People like Sepp Blatter and others in positions of power who fail to make the right decisions. After the Suarez and Terry incidents, Blatter said a handshake between the two players should be enough to settle an argument when it comes to racial insults! Just shake hands and walk away, he said. What an idiot! I hammered Blatter on Twitter for that. Here was the head of our game, and he obviously doesn't understand it at all. Other people criticised him as well and he had to backtrack. Hopefully he educated himself a little bit. A year or so later, in Italy, the AC Milan team walked off a pitch in solidarity with Kevin Prince Boateng when he was insulted by racist fans. First Blatter said Boateng was wrong to do it. Later, he invited him to Zurich and praised him. It would be nice to think Blatter

ON RACISM

finally understood the issue. But my impression was that was all public relations.

Here, Kick It Out and Show Racism The Red Card had their chance to shine but they didn't take it. They weren't alone.

4. TRUTH AND RECONCILIATION

'Deal with it...' What does that mean exactly? I've spoken about the shortcomings of individuals and authorities. But as a family we weren't too keen on some of the approaches on the other side of the argument either. It was an emotional time and some idiots were saying 'you should go round John Terry's house and beat him up' or 'send someone round to fuck him up.' I just got cross about that. Are you crazy? That's not the way to do things! That's not what we are about! We're not that type of family! Meanwhile, people in the black community were saying 'do this' or 'do that' or 'Rio has to do something politically.' But we never *ever* wanted to make it a political thing about blacks versus whites.

There were also plenty of discussions going on between black footballers about how to 'deal with' the situation. People like Jason Roberts and Darren Moore were passionate about getting more black people with powerful voices and status in the game to be involved with decision-making. I totally agreed that something had to change. In the past the FA have cherry-picked people they can dictate to and use as puppets. It would be better to have people inside the power structures who the black community can trust and respect.

#2SIDES: RIO FERDINAND

One of the reasons I agreed to work on the FA commission on the future of the national team was to understand the organisation better and to get closer to the people making decisions. Who were they? I wanted to identify them.

It also bothered me that, when it comes to questions of discrimination, there were no players of the current generation involved in making decisions. I'm talking here about players of every color and creed and culture. For example, when it came to my 'choc ice' tweet, why did the FA turn to Lord Ouseley as an 'expert'? The FA should have been consulting people who are closer to our generation and have a better understanding of today's language. Words that meant something in his generation have a totally different meaning for mine. They used his interpretation. When I went to the hearing, I said: 'Why is Lord Ouseley even part of this conversation? He's an old man who's got no idea what we mean.' But it wasn't his fault. He was asked a question which he answered in the most honest way he could, I'm sure. It's complex because there are many minority groups all with different voices and opinions and feelings. When you talk about inclusion you have to think about girls playing football and discrimination and exclusion against gay players. It all needs to be updated and I think the FA may be in the process of trying to do that. The problem is that as an organisation it is always reactive rather than proactive.

Some black footballers saw the Terry case as a chance to 'make a stand' and 'let people know we're not happy.' There was talk of setting up a separate organisation, a sort of black players' pressure group. I could see what they were getting at.

ON RACISM

But separatism of any kind just isn't my thing. I don't think segregation bodes well for the future. I don't want people cutting themselves off from each other. There has to be no boundaries; you have to be inclusive of everybody. That's the way I've been brought up. To me the John Terry and Luis Suarez cases had nothing to do with being pro black or pro white. I'm not pro black or white, or pro Jewish, or pro Muslim. I respect *everyone*, wherever they're from, whatever their culture. I'm not saying it because I'm a black guy. I'm saying: everyone, please just respect each other! That's all I want for my kids. I don't think it's a hard thing to ask for.

John Barnes, who I respect greatly, says it's possible for someone to make a racist remark without necessarily being 100 per cent racist. He says if someone says 'black bastard' it's not absolutely conclusive. The way he sees it, it might just be the emotion of the moment and first thing that came to mind. Back in the day I would have completely disagreed with that. I would have said there were certain totally unacceptable words and if a person says them, well, that's it: they are racist and I would write them off immediately. But John was a hero of mine when I was a kid. I don't agree with everything he says, but he made me think. Obviously, if someone makes that mistake a couple of times, then it's something in them. It's not a mistake. And I really don't understand how a person doesn't have a switch in their body, or a light that comes on and says, 'that one's a no-go.' Perhaps that person just never had discipline at home when they were growing up, or they're just ignorant. On the other hand, if it's just a one-off, maybe they do deserve the benefit of the doubt.

One thing I totally agree with John Barnes about is that racism comes from sheer ignorance. I used to say that football is a great tool for making people aware of racism – but it can't stop racism. If someone comes to the stadium and says something racist he knows he might be banned for a long time, so he'll be quiet during that 90 minutes – and then go somewhere else and be racist. It just changes his behavior in that very small context. In other words, football's not educating him to be a better person. That has to be part of a wider education and social education, so we need that education in the home, and the schools and in the media.

The only thing we wanted out of the whole John Terry affair was to get people talking about racism not in an antagonistic way but in a thoughtful way. We wanted people to understand that racism was still a problem. Everyone thought we'd dealt with it but it's not dealt with! It's still there! And we never attacked John Terry. We never said – and never will say – that John Terry is this or that. Never! That's why I couldn't understand why there was so much hatred directed at us. The media stoked up the idea of 'us versus them' but as a family we always said: this isn't about Anton or about John Terry. This is about racism as a whole. It's about the next generation. I don't want my children or anyone else's children to grow up thinking it's normal to be racially abused whether they're white, black, Indian, Asian… it doesn't matter what race you are. That was our whole approach. To borrow a Nelson Mandela-era idea from South Africa, what we wanted was not a court case but something more like a truth and reconciliation commission, something to create light rather than heat, a way to use the incident to help educate people.

But that never happened. We told the FA to deal with it quickly. The incident happened on a football pitch and should never have ended up in court. It was absolutely obvious what had happened and the FA should've dealt with the situation before a complaint even came in from a member of the public. It wasn't difficult. Go and see Anton; go and see John Terry; look at the video; make a decision. Simple. But the FA made it sound like it was the most complicated, difficult case they'd ever seen. And they passed the buck for almost a year.

England: Hoddle and Co.

We've wasted a generation
Or two

When England does badly in a World Cup the jokes start. They're all basically the same joke. After the 0–0 with Algeria in South Africa it was: *I can't believe we only managed a draw against a rubbish team we should have beaten easily … I'm ashamed to call myself Algerian.*

I love a laugh as much as anyone, but I want these jokes to be obsolete. I want England to be good again. I think we can make it happen, but to do that we need to understand where things have gone wrong in the past – and what's wrong now.

To play for your country is the greatest thing you can do as a footballer but most of my experiences were tinged with the feeling that we could have been doing so much better. England's biggest problem is that we don't produce nearly enough top-level players. Another is that we haven't worked out how the national team should play. The days when anyone thought we could do well with old-fashioned blood and thunder are long gone. But we've never developed a new philosophy. What is the 'English style' these days? No one knows. It's frustrating and after nearly 50 years of hurt, I reckon it's time we sorted it out. I'll explain more about my ideas on that in a later chapter. But first I'll give you my impressions of the England managers I played under.

By far the best was Glenn Hoddle. I was lucky enough to work with him in the late 1990s when I was still a teenager. He had a crystal clear vision of how he wanted us to play, and how to get us there and I still think it was a tragedy for us when he was sacked for his religious beliefs. If he'd stayed I would have been a different player – and a better player – for England.

Hoddle encouraged me to come out with the ball and sometimes even played me as a sweeper. He had a vision for me as a creative centre-back – not just defending but starting attacks, like I did at West Ham. He'd say to me, 'When you get the ball, drive out of the back, commit someone, go past them! Don't worry about leaving a gap – someone will fill in for you when you go forward.' It was refreshing.

I also loved his imaginative training methods. He'd talk to me about skills I'd done, and encourage me to do more: 'Try things. Don't worry about making mistakes. That's not a problem, as long as you don't make the same ones over and over.'

He was only just getting started, and I'm sure if he'd stayed he would have had England playing his way. It would have been good, progressive football but with a real winning mentality. Sometimes we'd play with three at the back,

ENGLAND: HODDLE AND CO.

other times we'd have four. Sometimes we'd go with four midfielders, sometimes five. All the players enjoyed it because it wasn't just about passing and attacking more; it was about playing with purpose, with a real focus on being flexible and tactically creative.

Glenn Hoddle contributed a great deal to my football education. He painted mental pictures so we could visualise the game in front of us. He also had a knack of simplifying things and breaking things down. The manager would say: 'If you come out of defence and take one of their midfielders with you it creates problems for them here, and here, and here … and when you move forward someone else in the team will drop in to your position, so don't worry about that.'

Hoddle would spot a weakness in our next opponent and gear training towards that. If their fullbacks were weak, we'd work for two or three days on how to attack them. He might box that part of the pitch in training and make us route all our attacks through that area. He was one of our greatest-ever technical players and his training mirrored the way he played: loads of fun skill stuff, and lots of keep ball and one-touch. One part of the warm-up was going through cones with the ball and having to chip it back, or keeping the ball up and volleying it back without letting the ball touch the floor. It annoyed some players who weren't great with their touch. Michael Owen used to moan his head off: 'Fucking hell, not this skill shit again.' His game was about scoring goals. He was brilliant at it, and that's all he wanted to work on. But I loved it – I'd happily do skills all day long.

Hoddle took me to the 1998 World Cup in France and even though I didn't play, he'd started to trust me and said he wanted me to build the defence around me. It's the only time I've thought to myself, yeah, I can see a future for England, I can see what he wants to do. He had a clear vision of what he wanted and you saw the beginnings of it at the Tournoi de France in 1997. By 1998 the team was starting to take shape: young players were coming through and we were on the cusp of getting really good. Then he got sacked. It killed us and I don't think we've ever recovered. Ever since, I've been hoping someone would come in and continue what he started but it has never happened.

Kevin Keegan took over in 1999 and I knew straight away he didn't fancy me as a player. Coming up to the European Championships in 2000, he came to my room and said: 'Listen, Rio, I'm not going to take you. You're a great player, and you've got a big future, but I don't think you've got the experience and I need to take experience.' Then he took Gareth Barry who was younger than me! Even more ridiculous was that he said 'if you were Italian, or Brazilian, or French you'd have 30 caps by now, the way you play.' I thought: 'Well you just spoke about the World Champions, the European Champions, and one of the best teams in the world ... But I can't get in the England squad!' Suffice to say I didn't get on too well with Kevin Keegan as a coach.

Before and after Keegan, Howard Wilkinson took charge for a couple of games and that was just bizarre. He was like a school teacher or an army sergeant. He had us out doing set pieces the morning of the game in a field next to the hotel

ENGLAND: HODDLE AND CO.

and all he wanted to talk about was set pieces. 'Set pieces win games,' he'd announce, and then he'd tell us the percentages of games won by set pieces and... well, I'm afraid he lost me completely.

Compared to those two, Sven-Göran Eriksson seemed a huge step up. When he was appointed in 2001 I thought, 'Wow, he's been a great manager in Italy, he must be cultured and sophisticated and we'll be back to the days of Glenn Hoddle again!'

I remember going to our first meeting with him. I was so eager and excited. I thought: what magic has he got to sprinkle on us? I came out and remember saying to Frank Lampard: 'That guy just made football sound more basic than any manager I've ever played for!'

The first conversation I had with Sven he said to me: 'I don't want my centre-backs running with the ball.' I couldn't believe it. But he was the England manager and I wanted play for England, so if he told me to lick his boots ten times in order to play for my country I'd have done it. Tactically he was very unimaginative: 'I want you to go here; I want you to go there. I don't want my centre-backs running with the ball. I want you to get the ball, pass it here.' But he was also charming and had a good, human side which created a nice atmosphere in the squad and meant we always wanted to play for him.

I think Sven was a bit over-awed by David Beckham. If truth be known, he was a bit too much of a Beckham fan. But, still, Sven was a genuinely nice fellow. I remember one time Wayne Rooney and I were on the massage table just after the story came out about Sven's affair with Faria Alam. The TV was on and, as we're lying there, Faria Alam appears on the screen. There were quite few people milling about and people coming in and out of the room. I was going, 'Look at her! I bet Sven ... I mean, can you *imagine?* I bet he was throwing her *all over the gaff!*' All of a sudden I notice it's very quiet and Sven, standing behind me, goes, 'Well, it wasn't *quite* like that'; he then starts to laugh, says 'Good night' and walks out. I'm lying there thinking: 'Oh God, what have I done?' while all the lads are cracking up. But that's what Sven was like: he made everyone feel comfortable. I liked him a lot and got on really well with him. Tactically, he wasn't sophisticated like I expected and he didn't bring us on; but maybe I was expecting too much.

Steve McLaren, who followed Sven, was a much better coach than people give him credit for. It's actually quite hard to say why things went wrong with him and we failed to qualify for Euro 2008. Again, when he first came in I was excited. I'd heard great things about him when he'd been at Manchester United and he'd been our trainer under Sven. One problem, I think, was he was just too pally with the players. There wasn't that distance you normally get between manager and players, like we had with Ferguson. Yes, sometimes we can be joking around, but at a certain point it's clear: 'I'm the manager, and this is how it goes.'

McLaren didn't have that. He'd call John Terry 'JT' and Frank Lampard 'Lamps', and play two touch with us during training. A lot of the squad saw that not as weakness, exactly, but as something strange: that's the kind of thing you do that

ENGLAND: HODDLE AND CO.

as a coach, not as a manager. With the best managers, I find, there's always a distance from the players.

But, again, Steve McLaren was a decent, good guy. He got hammered later for that interview he did in Holland where he spoke with a Dutch accent. But I didn't see anything wrong with that. I thought it was very human. I used to do something similar in training with foreign lads at United. It's a way of trying to help people understand me. If it can help them understand a bit better, I'll speak slowly and try to use their accent. My Dad used to work with a lot of Turkish people in the rag trade and he'd do that. He'd be like *'Sevela, come on, come on. Why you talking? Come on, please ...'* so they would understand him a little bit better. I respected that; it's a nice trait to have. But at the same time, managers seem to have to be a bit more resolute to succeed. I'm not a manager yet, so I don't know.

People criticised McLaren for his tactics but I'm not sure I'd go along with that. It's very hard to put my finger on why things didn't work. Stuff just seemed to go wrong, like in Croatia when the ball bobbled and went under Paul Robinson's foot. That was hardly the manager's fault! The truth is that we just didn't play particularly well throughout that qualifying tournament and I think the players have to take a lot of the blame for that. We didn't perform. It's as simple as that.

Then it was time for Don Fabio, who was appointed in 2007. I think Capello was the manager who disappointed me the most. He came to us with a sky-high reputation and I couldn't wait. He'd coached the AC Milan team I loved as a kid, with Marco van Basten and Gullit and Rijkaard and people like that. I knew he was going to be progressive – I mean, he'd been at Real Madrid. And Roma. He'd been everywhere, done everything, won everything. When he first arrived I asked him about the great players he worked with and he'd start talking about the Baresis and Maldinis. I thought: 'This is going to be so great! I'm going to learn so much! He's got all this fantastic knowledge and experience, he's going to bring great stuff to this team. Now we're definitely going to improve.'

And … what a let-down! He had us playing the most rigid, basic 4–4–2, with no deviating allowed under any circumstances. One game against Spain he had us playing with two central midfielders against the three best midfielders in the world. I thought: 'The game has evolved, man! This is not possible! Please get some bodies in here to stop us getting overrun!' It wasn't rocket science.

But what could we do? With Capello you have to just do what you're told or you're out. I should also stress that it wasn't my best period because I was struggling with my back problem and was injured a lot. You want everyone to see you in your best light, especially someone you've respected for years. Then again, I think most of the players felt let down. I remember Jamie Carragher being disappointed as well. He'd just come out of retirement from England, to work with this man. We expected ideas and creativity, but what we got was a stifling prison camp mentality.

Capello's attitude was 'I'm the boss and you'll do what I say all day, every day.' There was never much warmth. He seemed

ENGLAND: HODDLE AND CO.

to need to show us how strong and disciplinarian he could be and was so aggressive sometimes it was just ridiculous. There was a definite divide between him and his coaching staff and us, which we respected. But some of it wasn't very clever – like the way he chose the captaincy, giving John Terry and Steven Gerrard and me a game each. He made an absolute circus of the situation.

Part of it could have been a cultural problem; mostly, though, I just think he hadn't moved with the times. Playing 4-4-2 was getting us outnumbered in midfield *all* the time. Rubbish teams were passing the ball around us, like Algeria at the World Cup. They kept the ball better than us and played better than us.

I know people back home were expecting us to win the World Cup in 2010 but that was ridiculous. There was no *chance* of doing anything. Tactically, we were all over the place, and even if we'd got past Germany in the second round, our midfielders would have been exhausted by the quarter finals because of the amount of ground they had to cover. We never had any respite in any of the games because Capello would always be shouting: 'Press! Press! Press!' even when it was hot. I've got nothing against pressing; it's an essential part of the modern game. But you've got to be intelligent about it.

Remember, this is a team of players who've played a brutally hard season in the Premier League. Our league is so exhausting it leaves everybody knackered for the big tournaments. Look at the statistics for the distances our players run; the intensity and sheer number of games we play really works against us. By the time we get to the quarter-finals of a tournament, we're on our last legs.

Added to that, most of us are carrying injuries. That was certainly the case with every tournament I went to. In Japan and South Korea in 2002, I had a groin injury and I don't even know how I played a couple of the games. My main memory of that tournament is *treatment*. Treatment, treatment, treatment … you needed vigorous treatment sessions just to get fit for a game. I do think a Premier League season is harder than a season in any of the other big leagues – and we don't have a winter break like they do in Germany. It's just another thing that works against us.

We still could have done better under Capello. People talked all the time about how Gerrard and Lampard in the same team never really worked. I thought the solution was to drop one of them, or give them very strict instructions: 'This is your role; that's yours.' But no one ever felt strong enough to do that because they were such good players for their clubs and were among the best in Europe.

One thing Capello did get right, though, was when he talked about the England shirt 'weighing heavy' on some players. The media talked us up as 'the golden generation' but we certainly never gave ourselves that tag and it became a millstone. We'd have one good game in the run-up to a tournament and suddenly be favourites to win it. We'd go into a tournament thinking if we don't get to the final it's a failure. It magnified and built up the pressure to a ridiculous degree.

I've been on the bus after a game and heard senior players worrying: 'Oh no that's going to be four for me in the paper

ENGLAND: HODDLE AND CO.

tomorrow.' You laugh, but when you get to your room you think that's an England player saying that! How are we going to have a chance of winning if he's thinking like that? If a player's obsessed with what the papers will say about him, how is he ever going to go out and express himself? The answer is: he can't. He'll do the exact opposite and decide to take no risks at all. He'll think: 'If I misplace a pass ... that's a five.' So he just plays safe. The pressure is unique. Expectations are high when you play for Manchester United. But with England it's intense for small periods of time: heavier and much more concentrated. It's just too intense. The players wake up, read the paper every day, see that people back home are doubting them – but the same time demanding the world. Then you've got people saying: 'He should play ... he shouldn't play... he should be doing this or that if he's in an England shirt ...' It comes with the job. And I'm sure they get worse than that in Brazil or Argentina. You've got to be able to take that burden on your shoulders. Some players can, and some players can't.

History may judge that Roy Hodgson's most lasting achievement was to lower expectations of the national team to a more modest and manageable level. Then again, modesty isn't really the point of international football.

My relationship with him never really recovered from the incident in October 2012 when he got chatting to passengers on a tube train in London and casually mentioned that my England career had reached 'the end of the road.' He apologized after the story appeared in the papers but it was so disrespectful. The England manager simply cannot speak to the general public about stuff like that. Later, as I explain elsewhere in this book, I felt he mishandled the issue of my possible return after injury and the relationship with John Terry after the racial abuse case. In relation to the England team, none of that would have mattered if Hodgson had managed to get us playing well. But he didn't. At Euro 2012, I felt he under-used exciting younger players and was too defensive in his tactics. Watching Italy's Andrea Pirlo take us apart with a passing masterclass in the quarter final, the thought occurred to me that if he'd been English Hodgson and other England bosses might never even have picked him.

At the World Cup in Brazil, I felt Hodgson got it wrong again in his approach to mixing youth and experience, falling between two stools. The defence wasn't good enough, partly because he left out Michael Carrick and Ashley Cole, two players with loads of tournament experience. And he put too much responsibility on captain Steven Gerrard. I'd rather the manager had put all his faith in youngsters and given them valuable experience.

The bottom line is that instead of developing our own English style of progressive, clever football as we could have done, we've wasted a generation or two. We've had eight managers since Glenn Hoddle and there's still an air of being unfulfilled. We never seem to be quite good enough as a team and as individual players, we never produce enough moments of brilliance and we never found the right formula for the players we've had. The sad fact is that we're even further away now from achieving anything than when I first went to a World Cup 16 years ago.

Moscow, 21st May 2008

Go left
Go left
Go left!

In the video of the penalty shootout you can see all the Manchester United players standing together on the halfway line with our arms round each other's shoulders. I've got my arm round Michael Carrick. What you can't see is that I'm holding onto him just to stay on my feet. By the time Ryan Giggs walks up to take penalty number seven, my legs have gone to jelly and I think I'm going to be sick. It's my job to take penalty number eight and all I can think is: 'Please don't let it get to me. Please. *Please.*'

The penalties are as close as the match. Cristiano Ronaldo, our best player all tournament, stutters his run-up and misses. A few kicks later, John Terry has the chance to win it for Chelsea, but slips, hits the post, and doubles over on the wet grass. He looks like he's been folded in half. Everyone else scores: Owen Hargreaves puts his in the top corner; it's beautiful. Tevez scores too, and Nani and Anderson. It takes a lot of bottle for those two young players to go up there and take Champions League Final penalties. Now Giggsy is doing his little run and … he buries it! Beautiful. Only now I'm next. I'm not sure my legs will even work. Before my turn, Anelka steps up to take Chelsea's seventh. He has to score to keep them alive. On the video you can see me telling our goalkeeper Edwin van der Sar to dive to his left. I'm actually pointing and screaming: 'Go left! Go left! Go LEFT!'

So Anelka runs up.

And Edwin goes right.

Not only is it raining heavily, we're also drenched in history. It's been nine years since United won this cup, 40 years since the only other time we won it, and 50 years since Munich, when the Busby Babes died trying to win it. The thought of losing now is unbearable.

It's an all-English affair in Russia but it makes perfect sense for us to meet in the final because we're the two best teams in Europe. Neither side came into the game as favourites, but Chelsea had slightly had the better of things against us over the last couple of years. Every time I watch Didier Drogba he looks unplayable, but he doesn't generally do much against us. Tonight, however, he slapped Vida and got himself sent off.

We were better than Chelsea in the first half. Chelsea were better than us in the second. It was 1–1 at the end. We can't lose this game because we'll never hear the end of it. Two days from now we'll be meeting up with England: I can just imagine John Terry, Ashley Cole, Frank Lampard and Joe Cole arriving with winners' medals round their necks. I can't have that.

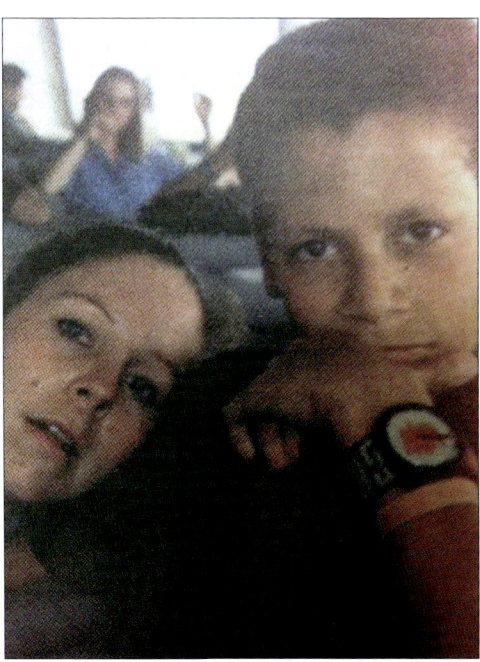

Above left: Me and my mate's mum, Sevily.
Above right: Me and Anton – big bro.
Below left: Me and Mum back in the day.
Below right: Me and Anton. © *Getty Images*

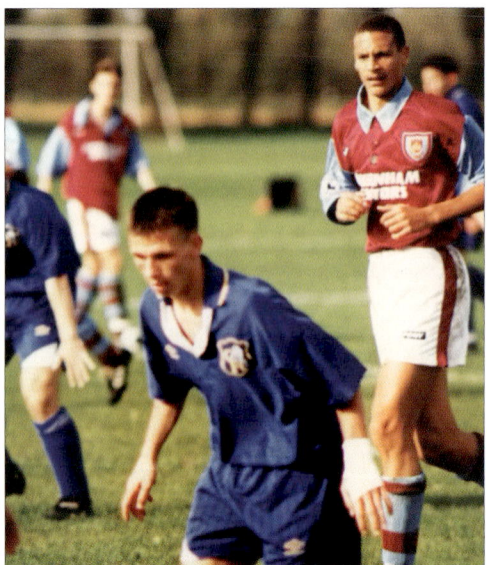

Above left: Me with the Hammers legend Julian Dicks.

Above right: Me vs Jody Morris (my old mate) as 16/17 year olds.

Below: Holding court as skipper at an England press conference! © *Getty Images*

I've had the opportunity to meet some great people over the years.

Above left: Ronaldo.

Above right: Lewis Hamilton. © Getty Images

Centre left: The late Nelson Mandela.

Below left: Me and Jamie at a #5 & Hublot party.

Below right: Pelé.

Me and the boys!

Above left: Me and Sir Bobby Charlton. © *Getty Images*

Above right: My last picture at the training ground, cleaning out my closet after 12 years!

Below: In the hoops at QPR. © *Getty Images*

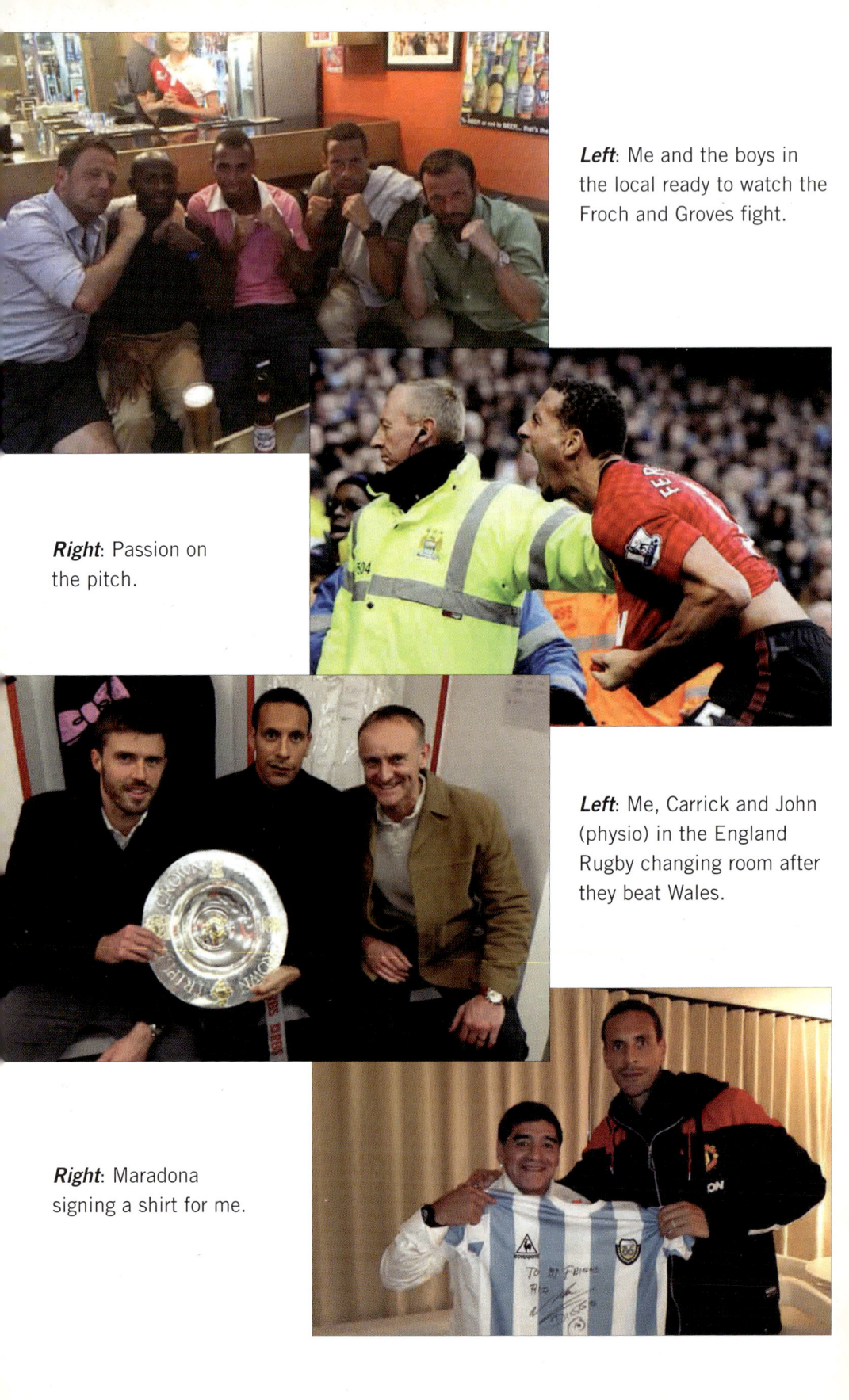

Left: Me and the boys in the local ready to watch the Froch and Groves fight.

Right: Passion on the pitch.

Left: Me, Carrick and John (physio) in the England Rugby changing room after they beat Wales.

Right: Maradona signing a shirt for me.

Me and Rebecca. © Getty Images

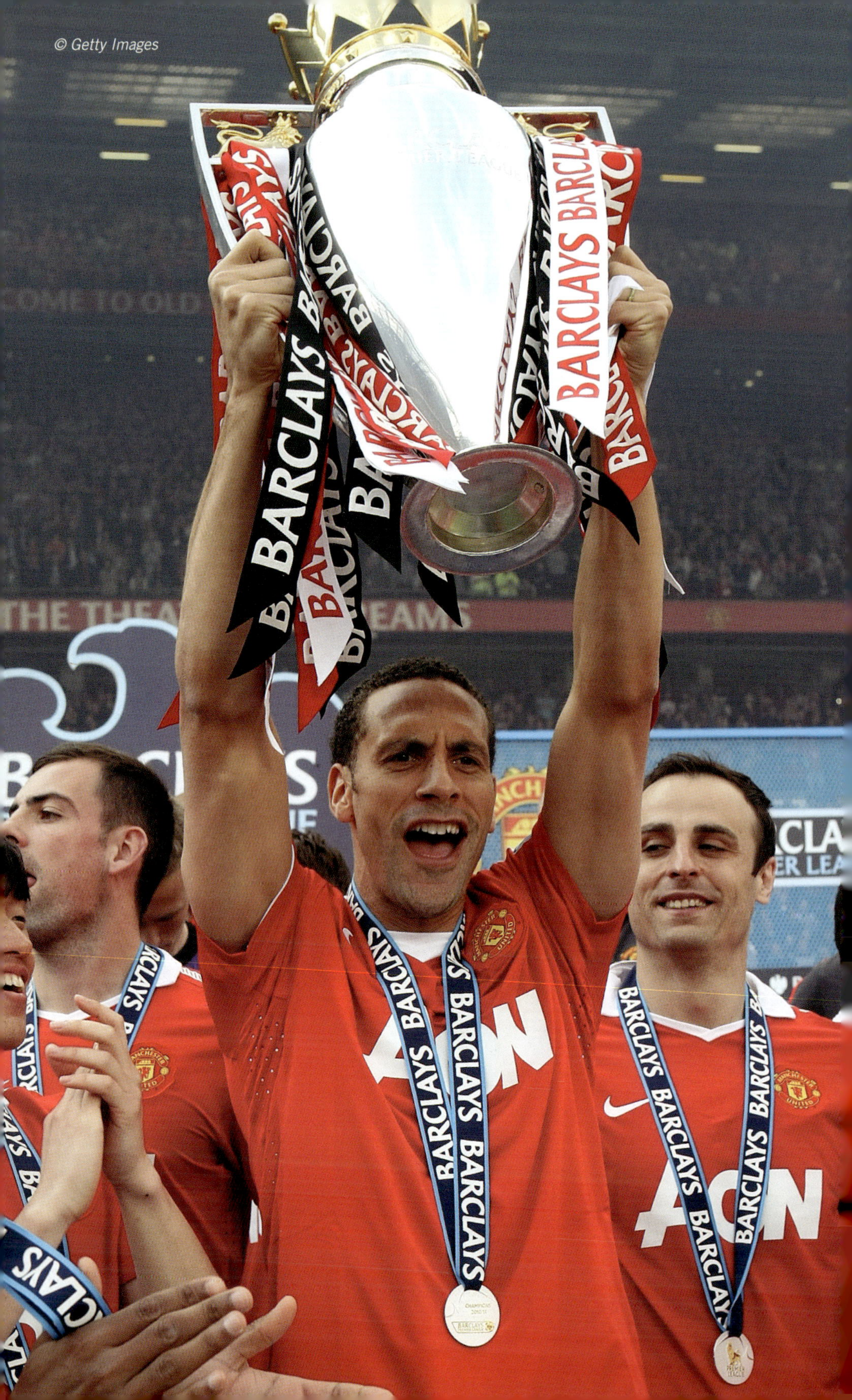

© Getty Images

MOSCOW, 21ST MAY 2008

Anelka runs up ... Edwin goes right.

There's really no way to explain how I feel in the split-second I realise Edwin has made the save. If you could bottle that emotion and sell it you'd be like the owner of a tech giant like Apple or something. It's ridiculous; it's my best moment; it's the best feeling I've had on a football pitch. It's something you dream about and think will never happen. I scream and run to Edwin, and jump on everyone. You don't know who to hug or who to kiss or who to cry with.

You start running around the stadium. Where's my family? They'd all come over for the game: my wife; Mum and Dad; Anton; my mates Gavin and Ray and Lorenz. You want to be with everyone. There are so many emotions.

Then you're standing there with officials and Chelsea go up to pick up their runners-up medals. You shake hands with your mates – with John Terry, with Ashley Cole (we were still mates then). You wish them well and stuff.

All of a sudden it dawns on me that I'm the captain and a few seconds from now I'm going to lift the trophy. I can't take it in – this is something other people do! I see Sir Bobby Charlton standing at the bottom of stairs before we climb them to pick up the big silver cup and ... and ... I well up. I can't help myself. Vida sees me and goes: 'Rio, man. Don't cry, man. Please don't cry.'

That helps me knock it off. I shake my head. No – I can't cry – I'm not going to lose it. Then I see Mum in the distance, clambering over all the chairs to get to where she could catch my attention. Clambering over people.

87

Clambering over chairs. She's going: 'Rio! *Riooooooo! Rioooooooooooo!!*'

Now I'm losing it, I'm definitely going to start crying. Vida leans in again and says: 'Rio. Don't cry, man. Please don't cry.' And that's it. I hold it together.

Before I lift the trophy, Sir Bobby Charlton, shakes my hand, pulls me to him and says to me: 'What a night! You will remember this day as long as you live, like I do mine. You've been great – now enjoy lifting it!'

The club secretary says 'Can you and Giggsy lift the trophy together?' And I say: 'Yeah, no problem. As long as I get my hand on it I don't care!' So we go up and we lift the trophy and it feels so good.

At the afterparty I'm absolutely steaming – probably the drunkest I've ever been in my whole life. There'd been rumours about Carlos Queiroz leaving so I'm on at him: 'Carlos, man, you can't leave us to go to Real Madrid!'

'I've got to explore it,' he says.

'No. No! We just won the Champions League!' I shout.

I have the same conversation with Ronaldo because there were rumours about him too. 'You can't leave! You just can't! Come on let's try and win this again. You've got to stay!'

The match was played in mid-evening UK time but locally, by the time we got back to the hotel it was one or two in the morning and the only food available was breakfast stuff. Our celebration dinner consisted of sausages, toast, and eggs and bacon. So we skip food and go to the bar.

MOSCOW, 21ST MAY 2008

I'm drinking anything anybody gives me. Everyone's taking pictures with the cup. I still can't believe we've actually won it. There's one bloke (I'd love to meet him again) who's in with a group of six fans. He's going: 'You can't drink, you bunch of footballers, you fairies.'

'OK then,' I say. 'You and me, drink for drink, let's see.'

Pretty soon I'm downing another six pints while he's surrendering at number three. 'That's it, I'm out! I'm out!' he says.

But Big Bollocks here carries on. I've taken over from the DJ; I'm dancing like a madman. Then my Dad comes and says: 'Rio, you've got to get up in an hour. Go and get changed.'

'What? What you talking about?'

He takes me up to the room. 'Dad, just get me another plane. You've got to book me another plane. I'm not coming back with the team.' That's how drunk I am.

'I'm going to sleep now, and I'm not waking up.'

'Get in the shower,' says my Dad. He puts me in the bathroom and turns on the water. Five minutes later he comes back and finds me in the shower ... *with my clothes on*.

'Dad, just book me a plane. I'm not coming.'

Somehow he gets me clean, dry, and dressed and out the room. I have no idea how. Onto the bus, and I'm still doing mad stuff and singing; the lads are crying-laughing.

Finally, a few hours later, me and all the other newly crowned champions of Europe land back in Manchester. And we're not just champions of Europe – we'd won the league too. It's a better Double than the League and FA Cup Double and the gaffer, being the gaffer, made sure we brought along the Premier League trophy for this very moment.

On the steps of the plane we step out and pose for the cameras. I'm holding the Premier League trophy; Giggsy has the Champions League trophy, and the gaffer is standing in the middle.

It's a picture I love.

Sir Alex Ferguson

Clarity
and
Energy

I didn't appreciate just how brilliant Sir Alex Ferguson was. 'You don't know what you've got 'til it's gone,' right? We took Fergie for granted but now I can see he was a genius. Coaches like Louis van Gaal talk about their 'philosophy'. Ferguson didn't make such grand declarations, but under him we played fantastic attacking, winning football. I'm often asked what his 'secret' was. There wasn't one thing – it was a mixture of things. He was a master of psychology, knew how to get the best out of every player and created an unstoppable winning mentality.

One of his principles was to give us freedom to express ourselves. He finished most of his team talks with: 'Now go out and enjoy yourselves!' It was never 'Do this, do that' because that can take away a player's flair and imagination. He gave people the confidence to try things and didn't mind if you made mistakes if you were trying the right things.

There was always a balance between discipline and giving us freedom; but at the same time, every player had to adapt to the general pattern of play which was rooted in Manchester United's history as a team known for exciting attacking football.

Dimitar Berbatov was an example of someone who just couldn't adapt or didn't want to. Berba, technically, is one of the best I've played with: a ridiculous amount of talent. But he wanted us to play a *tiki-taka* Barcelona passing game and I had arguments with him about that. I said: 'If that's how you want to play then go to Barcelona.' He wanted United to adapt to him, as Spurs and Bulgaria had done, but United doesn't adapt to any individual player.

Ferguson gave us the desire, the work ethic and the chance to go out and play with imagination in the final third. That was the stardust that he sprinkled over everything. He let us play without any kind of fear or pressure. If anything did go wrong – if we lost or the referee made a mistake – he always took the stress off us by creating an argument in the media, or picking a fight somewhere with someone. It distracted attention from what had done wrong on the pitch. I think José Mourinho learnt from that: as a manager, you've got to play the media. But later, at the training ground, Ferguson wouldn't forget. If we needed to be nailed, he would do that. But no journalist ever heard about it.

Psychologically, Ferguson knew exactly how to press people's buttons to get the best out of them. Somehow he always had me wanting to prove myself to him. I could count on one hand how many times he gave me compliments. He knew that if he praised me, I would probably get bigheaded. I wouldn't show it outwardly but inside I'd be walking around thinking, 'I'm the fucking *man*!' Instead, he had me always wondering if he even respected what I was doing. He was always talking about other players in the media and said nothing about me. But since reading his autobiography and hearing him speak after his retirement I realise that was part of his management; he'd identified certain traits in me that he didn't want to bring out.

One time, when Craig Bellamy was playing well, we were on the bus on the way up to Newcastle. The manager walked past me and flicked the top of my head, and went, 'That Bellamy has been telling Mark Hughes that he's going to destroy you. He reckons he's quicker than you, that you're not good enough to stop him any more.' I sat there and thought 'that cheeky little bastard.' So I went out and played Bellamy off the pitch – he didn't get a sniff all game. As I got back on the coach afterwards I said to the gaffer as we're leaving, 'Go and ask Mark Hughes now what he's got to say.' That's all he needed to do: he'd press your buttons like that – very simply – and it would get you going.

Every individual needs motivating in a different way. Sometimes he'd hammer Nani because he could get a bit complacent. More often, though, he'd build him up: 'Nani's unbelievable today. Keep getting the ball to Nani. I'm telling ya …' That was because forwards, especially wingers, are confidence players. 'Get the ball to Antonio [Valencia] because he's really on.'

One of the gaffer's masterstrokes in Robin van Persie's first season was to call a meeting about ten games in. The entire meeting was about getting the ball to Van Persie. 'Look at him! He's making all these runs and how come you're not seeing him? Are you lot not good enough? Am I going to have to go and find people who are good enough to get the ball into Robin van Persie? He's going to score you goals. Just get the ball into him. Wazza, when you get the ball, I want you to find him ... Scholesy, Carrers, when you get the ball ... Rio, when he's making his runs ...'

Looking back, I think, of course we were seeing him, what are you talking about? But he wanted to emphasise it, so everyone would focus a bit more. It created a mindset. He knew that if Robin gets chances, he scores goals. And if Robin was scoring goals we were going to win the league. Which is *exactly* what happened.

When preparing us for a game, everything was designed to keep us sharp, focused and positive. The main emphasis would be on *us*. Not much time would be spent on how we were going to stop the other team playing; Ferguson just gave us a few key points. For instance, against Arsenal, we used to always get very physical with them, overpower them and outrun them – then counter-attack quickly. He really wouldn't focus on their individual players but he would say 'Make sure you stay with runners. If they play one-twos, stay with runners.' That was it. It was a small detail but it was important because their main strategy was to play one-twos around the box and have people running off the ball. So: *stay with the runners.*

He also made sure we got on whoever it was that made them tick. For a long time that was Fàbregas. Later it was Arteta. The manager would say: 'Don't give him any time on the ball. You get on him. Smash him. Overrun them. We're quicker. We're stronger than them, play aggressive …' They never liked it. We beat them almost all the time.

Another thing he was clever at was hammering an individual to affect the team. He never suffered egos. When we played Benfica in Lisbon, Cristiano Ronaldo thought he had to prove to people in Portugal why he'd gone to United. The game became the 'Cristiano Ronaldo show'. He was trying to show his skills and nothing was coming off; we lost and afterwards the manager absolutely destroyed him. 'Playing by yourself? Who the hell do you think you are?'

Ferguson was brave to do that. He knew Ronaldo at that time was the key to us winning anything. If we were going to be successful and dominant he had to be in top condition. A lot of managers would have been scared of taking him on. I never saw England managers hammering Beckham like that, or Stevie Gerrard, or Frank Lampard, or Wayne Rooney. But Ferguson would go for anyone. It didn't matter if you were the main man, he'd open you up if you needed it for the team.

I remember Ronaldo getting emotional in the changing room after that game. He knew he'd played badly and he was upset by what Fergie had said. The reaction in the rest of the team was interesting too. Some people would be like: 'As long as it's not me I'm happy.' Looking back, I realise that it was Ferguson's way of saying to the whole team: It doesn't matter who you are, you'd better perform in the right way that helps the team.'

But at the same time Ferguson was a reader of personalities and someone like Berba couldn't really take that sort of treatment. He was a 6ft 3in, strapping lad, but his personality was such that if you hammered him, Berba would just go into his shell and wouldn't play at all. Ronaldo, on the other hand, used something like that to motivate himself: 'Right, I'll fucking show you …'

Sometimes, we might be a bit flat in a match but the manager wouldn't have anything to shout about, so he would pick on a little thing. Gary Neville might have let the ball run under his foot and conceded a throw-in so we'd come in and Ferguson would muller him. 'You've been playing for 15 years at a top level and you can't even control the ball!' Or he'd come in and say to Giggsy, 'You gave the ball away so much in that half.' Giggsy probably *wouldn't* have given the ball away any more than anyone else, but because he is the most experienced player, it makes everyone else think: 'I could be next. I'd better stay on my toes.' Even with me sometimes he'd say, 'You'd better sort yourself out, you've not even won a header!' And I'd go: 'Hang on I've had four headers and I've won three of them, and the other one I left because I knew the keeper was behind me and he covered it, so what are you talking about? You're wrong.' But he always had to have the last word. 'Well, we'll see that tomorrow on the video. Just fucking do what I tell you.'

I had a good and bad relationship with him. I could be fiery at times and quite vocal, and it didn't go down well sometimes. In 2010 we played Bayern Munich away in a quarter-final. The manager always preached that getting an away goal and winning 1–0 away from home is a good result in Europe; it means the other team have to score three goals to beat us at home in the second leg. So on this occasion, we'd gone 1–0 up; Rooney went off injured and the manager sent on Berba to try to finish the tie by attacking. On the pitch, I was waving my hands as if to say, 'what are you doing? This ain't the way we know how to play.' Somehow Bayern scored a couple of lucky goals. One was a deflection and another was right at the end of the game, making it 2–1 to the Germans. I'm on the pitch screaming and frothing at the mouth, and I walk down the tunnel still angry and emotional. I thought that tactics had gone against the principles he'd taught us and I couldn't get my head around it. I'm screaming, 'Why did we fucking change? That's why we fucking lost!'

As I came into the changing room, it was obvious he'd heard me. Gary Neville is trying to get me to calm down and as I walked through the door, I saw the manager standing right in the middle of the changing room, waiting for me. He just *unloaded*. 'Who the fuck do you think you are?' he screamed. By the time I sat down, he was standing over me shouting: '*I* make the decisions. *I'm* the fucking manager. Don't ever question me and my staff again.'

'You've brought us up to play a certain way, and you fucking changed it,' I said in reply.

'That was two lucky goals,' he shouted in my face. 'They were there for the taking. We should have wiped the floor with them. They were there waiting to be smashed and *you* let it go.'

Gary Neville was saying: 'Rio, calm down. Leave it, leave it.' But the manager always got in the last word: 'You're finished.' I forget what he said. It was just a blur of F-words really.

Gary Neville didn't even understand why I'd even said anything. 'What's the point?' he said after the row. 'You know you'll never win the argument.' I sat there thinking, well, someone should've said something here. Why is it just me? You all think it as well.

I kept thinking about it on the flight home and when I got home that night I couldn't sleep at all. I kept turning it over. Maybe I should've just sucked it in at the time and said what I thought in a quiet way later, when no one was there or maybe at the airport. It had been a big thing because I said it in front of everyone. So next morning I got up early, went to the training ground, got in at about 8.30am and went to his office. I knocked on his door. He just looked up and said, 'Come in. What do you want?'

'Listen. I've just come to say sorry. Maybe I should've spoken to you at a different time. The emotions of the game and losing just kind of got to me and I probably went too far.'

And he unloaded *again*! He went bananas. There was no respite. 'Who do you think you are? This isn't the first time you've questioned the tactics,' [referring to the Barcelona final in Rome].

I was trying to say, 'If you want someone to just sit here

and just accept everything all the time when we lose, then I'm not that guy,' but of course he didn't accept that.

That's how our relationship went. In fact, it's probably why we got on. We had spats, but I think, in the end, he realised I wasn't ever doing it just for my own personal crusade. It was for the betterment of the team. Sometimes, I crossed the line a bit and he had to kind of bring me back into line. Yet I always accepted that if I was wrong I would apologise. I think his mentality was that he would never let a player get the better of him. That's the way he led. But I think I earned his respect. Of course there was part of me that made me say to myself, 'Right. I'm going to prove this bastard wrong. I'm going to prove it to him.' That was Ferguson's genius: he had you wanting to prove something to him. I'm not criticising him at all; he was doing his job and I think he was probably right. I always respected what he was doing.

Another important thing was that he backed his players through thick and thin. That counted for a lot. There was the Patrice Evra and Luis Suárez incident; the John Terry situation involving my brother. And he backed me wholeheartedly over missing the drug test: he gave me a character reference and spoke in glowing terms about me. It is an essential part of Ferguson as a manager: when he believes his players are in the right he backs them to the hilt. That earns the trust and the desire to go out and work for him.

He was always doing surprising things to keep us on our toes. Right at the beginning of my Old Trafford career, I injured my ankle in my very first game, a friendly against Boca Juniors and their young star Carlos Tevez. Over the next five weekends, me being me as I was at 23, I over-indulged in Manchester's famous nightlife. On the fifth week, as I ran out for training, Fergie called me over and asked 'How are you doing, son? How are you enjoying Manchester? Have you settled in OK?' I was nervous because it was Sir Alex Ferguson I was speaking to. So I said: 'Yes, boss … erm … gaffer … I'm OK. I've been to a couple of restaurants here and there, you know, just taking things easy.' And very calmly he says: 'Does that include Sugar Lounge and Brasingamens?' Those were two of the biggest nightspots and I'd obviously been caught red-handed. Then he gives me one of his looks: 'I know everything, son, so let's get off on the right foot here. Now go and train.' My legs went! My new boss, the great Sir Alex, knew I'd been partying hard and being unprofessional. I thought 'Will he sell me? Will I even get a game now?' It was never mentioned again but he'd well and truly marked my card. One day we were winning 2–0 at halftime at Bolton which was one of the hardest places to go. It was one of the best performances I'd been involved in and we came in buzzing. He walks in, slams the door, and goes, 'You've got to fucking sort yourselves *out*! It's a fucking *disgrace*! You should be fucking 6–0 or 7–0. This championship could go down to the wire on goal difference so you better fucking make sure you score more goals.' He was digging out individuals: '*You've* missed chances … *you've* been slack with your passing.' Everyone was sitting there, shell-shocked. He walks out the changing room and everyone looks at each and says 'Was he watching that game or what? We were on fire; we were unbelievable.' We went out and I think we scored another two in the second half. After the game he said he was just trying to make sure we didn't get complacent and to understand that it's not just about this game, we've got a season to finish. We had to win the league.

Another thing he was big on was concentration. 'Make sure you're all concentrating, especially defenders.' And he would never, *ever* make an opponent out to be a great team, so we never went onto a pitch thinking: 'these guys are so good we've not got a chance.' He would always play it the other way. 'This is the worst Liverpool side I've seen,' he'd announce before the game. 'You ain't going to get a better chance to beat them.' Steven Gerrard had a few standout games against us but we very rarely let him dominate. That was because the manager knew he was their danger man and he knew we had to stop him and smother him. With Frank Lampard, Ferguson would say, 'Make sure someone follows his runs, because he can score a goal.' Or: 'Don't let Drogba bully you … if I see Drogba pulling that ball down and bullying any of you, I swear to ya …'

I think perhaps the biggest thing was that he never confused us with too much detail – just a few key points and a mindset that there's no doubt that we're going to beat the other team. If you go out with a clear, strong idea, you'll execute that in a more decisive manner. Clarity and energy: that's what he gave us. The truth is that football is not as complicated as people sometimes make out. Just win your individual battles, make sure your team is set up in a good shape, work harder than the other side, and be decisive in the final third and in your own box. If you do all that you have a good chance of winning games. People like to pretend there's a big mystique to winning football matches. But a lot of it is simple: don't make things too intricate, and let people play off the cuff a little bit. Management isn't easy, but people often try to overcomplicate. Don't get me wrong; tactics are important. But sometimes, the game takes care of itself.

Looking back, there's a moment that gives me particular pleasure. I scored our winning goal at Old Trafford against Swansea on 12th May 2013. It was a peach of a volley, I must say, but I didn't realize its significance until later. In the changing room I was next to Nemanja Vidić and he was just sitting there smiling at me. I said 'What?' He said: 'Don't you know, big man? You just scored the very last goal here of Ferguson's time as manager.' I honestly hadn't thought about it. I was just happy about scoring and winning. But when Vida said that it hit me! I had a big old smile for ages afterwards.

Wildebeest

We park our cars

We take it for granted in England that football coaches and managers give instructions, and players do what they're told. That was certainly the case with Ferguson. He would tell us stuff and we'd be quiet, accepting what he said and taking it as gospel. This is what happens: we're told exactly what to do, and we go along with it and trust the manager's judgment on a lot of things. But in other sports it can be very different. I remember speaking to Andy Farrell, the England rugby player and coach and I was amazed by what he described. Basically, when they have team meetings about tactics and stuff in rugby the players seem to run those meetings. The coaches say their piece but it's the players who make most of the running. Everyone gives their opinions and then they decide – as coaches and players together – how they'll play.

Whereas in football, we're all used to the tradition that the manager decides the tactics and the players adhere to what we're being told. I'm not saying which is the better method but I found it interesting. I mean, I've always been used to that and I'm comfortable with being told what to do. But I'd like the opportunity to be able to put my opinions forward without it being looked upon as being destructive. Usually, a player coming out of the pack and putting his own ideas forward is frowned upon. That's just been the environment we've been brought up in. It's no slant on any individual player – it's just how it is. It's been like that at every team I played in, even the England team. As football players we're creatures of habit, so we don't really question it. It's just what happens. I mean, we're allowed to have an opinion but everyone is very clear that ultimately it's the manager who makes the decision. But in rugby, if the players have an idea about something it gets fully discussed and their opinions are taken much more seriously. They have more of a say.

It must be weird looking at it from the outside but what people have to understand is that as football players we are treated like children a lot of the time. We are ushered and ferried around from 'A' to 'B'. When we go to airports, for example, we don't have to look for anything or think about anything – we just follow security and follow people telling us what to do. We're like a herd of bleeding wildebeest. None of us knows where we're going or what we're doing; we just follow each other. That's it – everything's on the board. We're told what to do at every stage. All we've got to organise is making sure we get there transport-wise – that's it. Just turn up to the meeting place. Once we get to that meeting place and park our cars, we're in the hands of the club, and the club takes care of every single little thing – no stone's left unturned.

All that's done for a reason – so we can concentrate solely on playing football. But it also means we're treated a bit like babies. There's an obvious downside: as soon as you take players out of that environment, some of them can't handle it because they're used to being wrapped in cotton wool and having everything taken care of.

But maybe it's the more effective model. Sometimes in a team you get divisive characters coming out and that ruins it for everybody. Or you get a manager that lets the changing room control and dictate what happens, and that can be successful. But ultimately in football, if the manager's not leading, then the players generally don't become successful. That's what I've noticed: I think there are players who will make decisions on the pitch, but ultimately when you have the manager dictating from the top, that's when the teams tend to do best. You might get the odd team that does it the other way around but, over a sustained period of time, I think you need a leader. That's the manager and he *leads*. Some people have argued that the role of managers can be almost irrelevant, that results are mainly down to the players on the pitch, and the manager's main function is to get sacked and be the scapegoat when results start to go wrong. I think it's a bit of both.

In my experience, the way a manager sets up his team – from a psychological point of view – is massive. Once you get on the pitch, then it's up to you to produce the goods and execute what the manager has put in front of you and prepared you for. The psychological aspect is huge.

On Balance

Do you really
Do ballet?

I've never been one to be boxed in by other people's prejudices. Who ever did gymnastics on my estate? No one. But I enjoyed it so I did that and it led onto something else. Someone spotted me doing gymnastics for Southwark in the London Games and thought I had potential as a dancer; they offered me a five-year scholarship at a ballet school on the other side of London, in Farringdon.

We didn't have enough money to get me from Peckham because it was an expensive long journey, over the bridge, across the water, so my Mum used to do fund-raisers. She organised little charity events to raise money for me and another two guys to go. So I ended up going each week and it was great. At first I went because there were lots of girls there and loads of different people to meet – it was more an adventure than anything else. But I really enjoyed it for the first two or three years. Then it started to be a little bit of a drag, I didn't enjoy it at the end. But I kept going because my Mum and Dad had put so much into getting me there.

I don't think in the long run I would have made it as a dancer, though I think I could have done something in the performing arts. Maybe as an actor – I was always into that kind of stuff. But being a ballet dancer is a really tough skill. They said I didn't have long enough hamstrings to have been a professional but learning to dance there left me in good stead in terms of balance and flexibility, and I'm sure it helped my movement later as a footballer. A lot of people don't realise how physically difficult and demanding ballet is. If you've seen *Billy Elliot* you know there's a kind of prejudice against it, but dancers have to work at least as hard as footballers, maybe harder. I had to put up with some stupid comments. People found it a bit bizarre – 'Do you really do *ballet?*' At first I didn't even tell people because I was quite young and I didn't know how people would react. It wasn't that I was embarrassed – I just didn't want to have to answer any questions.

But I was comfortable. I told a few of my close mates and they never said anything and after that I didn't care. Because I was quite a boisterous lad and quite cool within my group of mates when I was at school, no one really pressured me or was bothered by it. Maybe someone with a less outgoing personality might have had a harder time. I mean it shouldn't be a problem, should it? But that's just the way society is.

People often commented that on a football field I had a slightly different way of moving. Alex Ferguson talks in his book about me being 'graceful, balanced'. When I was a kid I was never into the traditional English hustle and bustle. Maybe that's because I played midfield. And, unlike other defenders, I was always thinking about the attacking elements rather than the full-blooded defensive stuff. I didn't enjoy heading the ball or making big tackles; I got my joy from doing skills or scoring or making a nice pass.

A lot of the way I moved on the field might have come from doing gymnastics and the ballet. Certainly I've never consciously tried to change the way I play to make myself look better. It was just natural to me. Maybe I'm just fortunate. But I think ballet contributed: I think it gave me a slightly different awareness of my body from other players.

Barça

If I stayed there would be trouble
And if I went it would be double

We lost to Barcelona in two Champions League finals and I still have nightmares about it. The two games, Rome in 2009 and Wembley 2011, were so similar they've blurred together in my mind as a single trauma. Both times we went into the match as champions of England and one of the best teams in Europe and on both occasions we were destroyed. Both times I went on holiday afterwards and couldn't even remember winning the league a few weeks earlier. Winning the league is a huge achievement, but all I could think about was how Barcelona had taken us apart. Was it my fault? Could we have done better? Flashbacks would hit at any moment. One time I was lying on a beach, soaking up the sun, listening to the waves. I'd just cracked open a cold beer. I was having a fantastic holiday with my family and ... BANG! All of a sudden I saw the Barcelona players celebrating. All the images from the game started playing in my mind like a video loop. I sat there thinking, please, just get out of my head!

Generally I don't remember our victories as clearly as our defeats. I think much less about the trophies we won than the ones that got away. Those two games haunt me more than all the rest. We weren't just beaten; we were *embarrassed*. It never happened to us before, and it never happened after. Don't get me wrong, Barcelona were the best side I played against; they had some of the best players that have ever played football. But I still believe that out of the two finals, we should have won one. If we hadn't played the way we did, I think we would have done.

After the first match, I remember the manager talking to us in the changing room. 'Listen,' he said, 'you were beaten by the better team today. You didn't turn up. You didn't perform. You didn't play.' He hammered us a bit – it was all the things you'd expect him to say. Then he said, 'Just make sure we're back here next May and fucking beat this lot because they'll get to the final again next year and you've got to make sure we're here to meet them.' So we knew what we had to do. We had to get back and right a wrong. It took us both a couple of years to meet again and we didn't right the wrong. But at least we got back. I don't think there are too many teams who would have recovered at all.

You probably remember the Rome game, when Barcelona won 2–0. What you might not remember is that we went into that match as favorites. We were reigning European champions and Barça had changed a lot since they'd won the competition in 2006: Frank Rijkaard, their manager, had left; some of their biggest stars like Ronaldinho and Deco had left. A new side was emerging under then-new manager Pep Guardiola.

It was an evolving team really. We'd beaten them in the semi-final the year before but we certainly didn't take them lightly. In the first ten minutes our tactics, which were to meet them high up the pitch and attack quickly, seemed all right. If we'd finished a couple of early chances, the game could have been different. Ronaldo had one and Ji-Sung Park had a chance that Piqué cleared off the line. Then Samuel Eto'o scored and after that it was just one-sided. They played the tiki-taka we now know all about, while we were wide open and just chasing shadows.

The most devastating thing about Barcelona that night was their confidence in possession. They had three of the best midfielders in Sergio Busquets, Xavi Hernández, and Andrés Iniesta, all great technicians, and they just strangled us with the ball. But they never passed just for the sake of it: everything had a deeper purpose. Lionel Messi, who was just emerging as the world's best, gave us hell as the 'false nine' and their wingers, Thierry Henry and Samuel Eto'o, played high and wide. Because we were trying to play on the front foot, we were caught between wanting to get forward but having to stay back to stop their runners. What was the best way to deal with Messi? He played from deep but if I went chasing him, I'd leave a hole for their midfielders and wingers to exploit. Should I stay or should I go? I never knew. Gaps opened and Messi exploited the space between our lines.

I think one of our problems heading into the game was that Sir Alex thought Barcelona would be like Arsenal. Both teams liked to attack and had technical midfielders who liked to pass around you. We'd thumped Arsenal in the semi-final, and the 4–1 battering we gave them at their place really felt like a case of men against boys. I think maybe we got a little bit carried away by that result; we didn't realise how much better Barcelona were. Their play was more structured; there was a real philosophy behind everything they did. They were a good few levels above Arsenal. Unfortunately we only found that out on the night.

What really hurt afterwards was feeling we hadn't played to our strengths. The style we'd developed over a period of years against the best teams in Champions League games was more counterattacking than attacking, and I thought we should have played that way against Barcelona. In 2010, José Mourinho's Inter Milan beat them with a defensive game and I think we were better and stronger than Inter. We never used to park the bus, and we didn't sit too deep. But we did like to sit; we'd keep a good shape with two banks of four, soak up pressure and then hit fast on the break. We had two important principles: no gaps between midfield and defence. When we won the ball the manager always told us to play the ball quickly into our dangerous wide and forward players.

So that's how we normally played, and we had players who were perfect for it. We were solid and strong at the back, and direct and clinical in our finishing. With guys like Cristiano Ronaldo, Wayne Rooney and Carlos Tevez up front, we broke records. In our best years, if anyone came to Old Trafford and played two strikers and two central midfielders, we were rubbing our hands, licking our lips thinking, 'Wow. This could be anything. This could be like 4–0 or 5–0. How dare they come to Old Trafford and disrespect us? We'll show them.'

The final at Wembley in 2011, when we were supposed to put right what had happened in Rome, turned out to be even worse. We had a two-week lead-up to the game and the manager thought long and hard about how to play. His plan was basically to do what we'd tried and failed to do in Rome when we'd been derailed by their early goal. The idea was to stop Barça dominating us by dominating them: attack would be our defence.

Sir Alex asked Vida and me and a few of the other senior players if we were happy with the tactics. We weren't really, but we're professional players; we want to do what the manager asks and he was a great manager. So we went with it. And lost 3–1. The score sounds respectable but it was hardly even a battle. We couldn't attack because we hardly ever had the ball, and at the end we came off the pitch embarrassed – they were head and shoulders above us.

Again, the most painful part of it was that we never got to show our qualities. We'd won back-to-back league titles; we'd been in three Champions League finals in four years. Yet here we were, getting taken apart in our own country. It was some coming down to earth for our players to be mauled like that at Wembley in front of our fans. It was particularly hard for Edwin van der Sar because it was his last ever game.

Tactically, the 2011 game was another disaster for us. As defenders, we never got to grips with Messi at all. Most of the time he played deep, well away from us. Then he'd suddenly ghost into the box and you couldn't catch him. I thought:

'That is fucking special. That is different. You're not going to see that ever again in your lifetime.'

Again, we had the impossible problem: stay back or go out and try to stop him. As defenders in England we thrive on contact. Look at Steve Bruce's nose – it's all over his face! That represents battle. Bruised ribs, broken ribs, knees, back … everything usually hurts after a game because you're fighting with forwards. But we barely even had a sweat on after that game. Normally you dictate to their forwards, but with Barcelona it was the opposite: they took the power out of our hands and dictated almost everything. I remember coming off at the end and saying to Vida: 'What the *fuck* just happened?'

We tried to find the answers in the game and in the second half I was almost playing in midfield some of the time, trying to go after Messi. The problem was, the minute you went out, their runners saw it, and Vida would be left alone with guys coming towards him from all angles. Barça posed questions we hadn't been asked before, and we didn't have answers. But if we'd played the way we were accustomed to playing I still think it might have been different.

When people talk about that Barcelona team they usually focus on Xavi, Iniesta and Messi. For me, though, the real killers were the wingers, Pedro and David Villa. They were fast and skilful, and played almost ridiculously high and wide, looking to get behind us. Since we wanted to take the game to Barcelona, our midfielders and forwards kept going forward, but the defence was pinned back by the danger of the wingers. If we'd all gone forward they'd have picked us off and it could have been a rout. Pedro was disciplined, intelligent and always did the right thing for his team; he never showboated or did flashy skills. For me, he was the one who really made them tick: he was also one of their best at pressing the ball and was so aggressive the whole team followed in behind him.

In his autobiography, Sir Alex criticises Vidić and me a little bit for those two games, saying we wanted to sit back and defend space rather than come out and pressurise Messi. As I've explained, I don't think that would have worked. But I can't be too critical of the boss. If I was being honest, I'd say, yeah, tactically he did get it wrong, but I think that's understandable. He feels the romance and history of the club deeply and I think he worried that United's tradition might be made to feel inferior to Barcelona's tradition. Like us, they're known for stylish attacking football. It's the Cruyff way of playing which they've brought all the way into the present. Guardiola's team was almost a reincarnation of the 'total football' of the 1970s. People raved about how good and beautiful Barcelona's tiki-taka was. But if we'd played defensively, where would that have left the history of United?

We have our own fantastic tradition: the Busby Babes, Best, Law and Charlton, 1968, all the great teams through the 1990s up to our own time. I think that's what drove the manager. He thought: I want to win our way, meaning the old Manchester United way, which was all about attacking, taking risks and meeting opponents high up the pitch. He let his heart rule his head, which isn't a bad thing sometimes. He was hurt at least as much as the players. To get to three finals in four years and only win one of them? He'd never have seen that in his wildest dreams.

What counts for me more than comments in his book is what Sir Alex said to us privately and from the heart in 2013. For me, it's one of his great moments. We were playing Real Madrid and before the game, during his team talk, he went back to those two Barcelona games. He opened up and said he thought he'd got our tactics wrong in both finals.

I'm man enough to admit that I didn't play well enough in either game. I think all our players would say the same thing. We're not stupid; we're not selfish enough to think, 'Oh, it's the manager's fault.' We didn't carry out his instructions as well as we could have done. Then again, he was asking us to do something different from normal. So whose fault were those defeats? Maybe the blame was a bit of a 50-50. Or maybe it was no one's fault. Barcelona, after all, were brilliant. But those games haunted us. On that day the manager took responsibility; he took the blame. It was one of those occasions that showed you the value of the man and why he is held in such high regard. Sir Alex is not just a great winner but he has a decency and a strength of character. What he said that night made me respect him even more: 'I'm not going to get it wrong this time against Madrid and trust me, believe in what I'm doing.' I was impressed and moved and felt that a burden had been lifted from my shoulders. It made me want to run through brick walls for him even more.

On Gay Footballers

Society has changed

Football's attitude to gay players is out of tune with the rest of society. I was impressed when Thomas Hitzlsperger came out, but it would have been much more powerful if he'd come out when he was playing. I know it's easy for us to say, but it would have been great. We often talked about it in the Manchester United changing room. We'd say 'Listen, man, based on the polls that are done and the latest research – there must be one amongst us who's gay. Come on. Who is it?' It was just a laugh but the feeling that came out was always that we wouldn't be bothered if there's a gay man in our dressing room. I'd rather someone come out and told me this: 'Listen, I'm gay, man.' I'm not going to not talk to him or treat him any differently. That was the common feeling even in a macho dressing room like ours: just be the person you are and don't change and we'll be fine with that. Whether you're gay doesn't bother us. As long as you're playing football to the best of your ability, and you're helping us win things, who cares?

#2SIDES: RIO FERDINAND

My general feeling is that I don't think someone coming out as gay would destabilise a changing room at all. What would probably happen is that if you came out and said you were gay, it would be like coming out and saying I've had a hair transplant or any other personal thing – you'd get banter but nothing nasty. It would be tongue-in-cheek like when Wayne Rooney got his hair transplant. That's how changing rooms are: it's part and parcel of it. 'Oh no, it's going to rain today,' we'd say, 'What's going to happen with his hair? It's going to be everywhere ... he looks like Bobby Charlton and he's only 21.' Anything at all that sticks out about someone becomes a thing you tease them about. When Cristiano Ronaldo wore tight jeans, we use to destroy him: 'We can see the veins in your bollocks, what's going on?' But he would laugh and come back and say 'You English guys don't know fashion, what are you talking about?'

If someone announced they're gay, I'm sure the atmosphere in the changing room would be like: 'Do we say anything about it?' and then I'm sure after 10 minutes someone would make a joke and it would break the ice and then everyone would just be getting on like normal. How refreshing that would be for football and everything. It would show people that we've all got a common goal and that is to win. It doesn't matter what colour you are or what you're into, if you're gay or not, or how you want to dress, whatever you want to do in life; as long as it's not going to get in the way of winning, it's all fine. I'm also guessing it would free up a lot of energy that is presumably wasted in people feeling they've got to hide something as fundamental about themselves.

ON GAY FOOTBALLERS

Look at Hitzlsperger. Maybe if he'd come out sooner he could have got another 15–20 per cent out of his career. If he didn't have that stress and pressure of hiding and feeling apprehensive about showing his true feelings, you never know, he might have had 100 caps for Germany. We remember the tragedy of Justin Fashanu – but he was playing more than 30 years ago. I'd like to think being gay in football today would not affect a player's chances in Britain in this day and age. Society has changed and football is a part of that.

On Being Captain

It's a beautiful thing
But I'm not bitter

People think it's just an armband, but being a captain really is a beautiful thing. You lead your teammates out onto the field; your chest puffs out with pride. I loved the role and it was an unbelievable responsibility and privilege to be captain of Manchester United and England. You think of some of the great players who've gone before you.

I just wish I could have done it a bit more often. In one case I felt uncomfortable about doing it at all. At Leeds, when I was 22, I felt very awkward when David O'Leary gave me the job. It was the way he handled it: Lucas Radebe was captain when I arrived; he was a top respected player, a top respected man and a great fella at the club. But he'd also had a lot of injuries. I'd only been at the club a couple of months when the manager pulled me out of the physio room. I found myself standing in the corridor with him and Lucas was there as well. O'Leary went: 'Rio um … Rio, I'm going to make you captain.' Dropping a thing like that on my toes right in front of Lucas! I didn't know what to say. Lucas was typically gracious. He smiled and said, 'Rio, you're the man, and you're the one to lead the club now. I want you to be the captain.' I just stood there. I said 'Sorry, man … I didn't want … I didn't expect it to be like this … ' I was embarrassed.

Leeds had a special parking space for the captain. But I didn't want to use it because I felt it was out of order. It became quite a thing. Some of the lads hammered me over it. When I arrived each morning guys like Lee Bowyer, Gary Kelly, Jonathan Woodgate, Michael Duberry and Robbie Keane would be standing there doing a commentary: 'Will he do it today? Is he going to park there? He is …. He is … He *isn't*!' At lunchtime, if I went up first for food, some of them would go: 'Lucas, to the back! You're nothing now.' The lads made it uncomfortable. But it was funny too. Then one day Lucas came to me and said, 'Rio, just park there, please. I want you to park there. You deserve it. You're the captain now.' And eventually I did.

But later, there were times with England and Man United when I thought I should have been captain and it didn't happen. I can hardly be bitter about it, though; everyone has their disappointments, moments in their career where they feel undervalued. No one has a right to be captain and my attitude was always the same: as long as I'm playing and I'm winning how can I moan? With England we didn't actually win any honours, but to be captain of your country is a massive honour in itself. I was devastated when I finally got my opportunity to lead the team at the World Cup in South

ON BEING CAPTAIN

Africa and I got injured; I felt as if it had been snatched away from me.

I was disappointed, though, when I was overlooked by Fabio Capello at the beginning of his time in charge. I felt the way he handled it was almost guaranteed to upset someone. He kind of put me, Steven Gerrard and John Terry on trial, giving us a match each to see how we coped, then finally picked John. It would've been far better if he had just come in and said, 'He's captain.' Bang. That's it. Or if he had asked the players, or taken an anonymous vote. I didn't see what he could have learnt from those three games. The problem for me was that you couldn't help get your hopes up and then get disappointed. It's one of the biggest things in football. So I was gutted. But I made sure I didn't let it affect my demeanour around the camp; I just got on with things.

At Manchester United there were times when I thought I could or should have been captain – but the hardest moment was when I actually was. It was the day we won the league on the last day of the season at Wigan in 2008: I'd been acting captain all season because Gary Neville had been injured for a long time. We won the game 2–0 and it was a fantastic feeling. Just after the match but before we went out for the silverware, I was sitting in the changing room when the manager comes to me and says, 'Ah, can you ... um ... let Ryan Giggs pick up the trophy?' My heart just sank, and I was like, 'Oh no ... this is a childhood dream!'

The most important thing is winning, of course. But to do it as captain puts the icing on top. I didn't say that, of course; I just said 'Yeah, no problem. It's fine. Great. Go. No worries.'

I understand why Sir Alex did it. Giggsy had won the league for … I don't know … the trillionth time. I think it was his tenth one. So it was a landmark moment for him. But I was thinking: 'Fucking hell, man … this is only like my third or fourth one. And how many more times am I going to get the chance to lift it as captain?' (None, as it turned out.)

So it was a bittersweet moment. Perhaps Sir Alex was thinking 'Rio doesn't need this so much because he's going to be around for a long time and win a few more of these.' But you never know what's around the corner. Over the next year, whenever I saw Giggsy with the trophy on the Sky match-day programme credits I thought: 'I might never get a moment like that.' I carried on being captain for a couple of years while Gary Neville was out with his injury problems. But when Gary retired I started getting injury problems of my own and the captaincy passed me by. My mate Vida got the gig and did a great job.

Giggsy never said a word about Wigan until, in the programme for my testimonial game, he acknowledged I'd given up that moment for him and he said he appreciated it. I appreciated what he said and it softened the blow. In any case, I can't complain too much; I got to lift the Champion's League trophy in Moscow a few weeks later and the Club World Cup Championship the following season. I've never been one to disgruntle my teammates; the well-being of the team is always more important than how you feel as an individual.

The Nice Guy

Mixed messages and low-fat chips

Just before Manchester United sacked David Moyes, I heard a journalist on the radio try to explain the crisis. There had been loads of discussion all over press, TV and social media, most of it ill-informed. But this explanation struck me as particularly bizarre because of the guy's tone. He was talking as if he was speaking the gospel truth – and at least half of what he was saying was complete bollocks!

'The club is not going to make the decision until Thursday ... the players won't play for the manager any more ... they've started calling him "eff-off"...'

What? As I listened I thought: Where *are* you getting this rubbish information?

On television the same week Roy Keane told the world the players had 'let the manager down.' I thought: 'Who do you know at Manchester United these days? Tell me! Who do you know? Who do you talk to? You left years ago!'

Other people even claimed we deliberately played badly through the season to get the manager sacked. Crazy! Maybe journalists think: 'I don't fancy this editor geezer so I'm deliberately going to write rubbish this weekend … and he'll get the blame!' But I don't know any players who'd ever down tools like that. At United it would be unimaginable to even think it. We were going to give 100 per cent for whoever became manager after Fergie, because that's the only way we know; we want to win, so we'll give the boss everything.

I was actually very optimistic when David Moyes arrived. Sir Alex was a great leader of people, and brilliant at judging people's character. Naturally, we all trusted his judgment. I think he identified with David Moyes purely on human qualities – and he was right. As a human being I think David Moyes is close to perfect. I like him: he's a real nice fellow, a genuine guy. His desire to succeed, his work ethic, his integrity are all fantastic. He's honest, trustworthy and passionate, and I totally see why Sir Alex warmed to him. Moyes was never going to be some fly-by-night manager who'd leave when it suited him; if he'd been successful he'd have stayed as long as the club wanted.

No one could have worked harder: Moyes was always the first one into the training ground and the last to leave. He is a true football man; he tried his best, and I can see why he got the opportunity. He'd proved himself at Everton; he consolidated them as a consistent top half of the Premier League team. But getting that opportunity and taking that opportunity are two different things.

Moyes never solved some of the football problems he faced. He brought ideas and tactics, which had worked for him at

THE NICE GUY

Everton, but didn't adapt to the expectations and traditions of Manchester United. He tried to impose a vision but never seemed to be completely clear what that vision should be. Unintentionally, he created a negative vibe where, with Fergie, it had always been positive.

I think he was entitled to bring some of his staff from Everton but it was an absolute mistake not to keep United stalwarts like Mick Phelan who knew all the quirks and sensitivities of the players. It meant Moyes missed a lot of the subtleties about players and the culture of United. But I have to stress, we all wanted to work with him and do well for him. It wasn't like Brian Clough going to Leeds and pissing off all the players by telling them to stick their medals in the bin. It was nothing like that!

It wasn't even that Moyes made one big mistake; it was an accumulation of mistakes. He slowly lost us. I didn't enjoy playing under him: long before the end, I'd decided to leave the club if he was going to stay. But I found it all fascinating. I learnt a huge amount. It made me appreciate a lot of things about Fergie I'd taken for granted. If I ever become a manager the experience of my last season at United will stand me in good stead.

The league table never lies. In 2012–13 we won the league by 11 points. I was so proud; I'd come back from my injury problems, had one of my best-ever seasons and was picked for the PFA [Professional Footballers Association] team of the year. Under David Moyes I suddenly found myself out of the team and we finished seventh, 22 points behind City. I can see why the new man wanted to put his own stamp on things. But if it ain't broke…

A lot of the time it felt as if he was just rubbing our fur the wrong way.

Like with the chips. Footballers are creatures of habit, and for as long as I can remember at Manchester United it was a ritual that we had low-fat chips the night before a game. We loved our chips. But Moyes comes in and, after his first week, he says we can't have chips any more. We weren't eating badly. In fact you'd struggle to find a more professional bunch of players than the ones at Manchester United in the summer of 2013. We were fit, had self-discipline and looked after ourselves diet-wise. Then suddenly, for no good reason we could see, it was 'no chips'. It's not something to go to the barricades over. But all the lads were pissed off. And guess what happened after Moyes left and Ryan Giggs took over for the last four games of the season? Moyes has been gone about 20 minutes, we're on the bikes warming-up for the first training session without him and one of the lads says: 'You know what? We've got to get onto Giggsy. We've got to get him to get us our fucking chips back.'

Here's another tiny thing we were irritated by: the pre-match walk. Moyes had us going for 10-minute walks together the morning of a game. We'd never done it before; no one enjoyed it and no one liked it. He never asked us about it. Maybe it's what he did at Everton, but we were all going: '*Why* are we doing this? What's the point?' It wasn't helping us at all; we were only doing it for him.

I know some people will think we're being prima donnas

about these sort of things. They think: 'Fucking footballers! All that money! What have they got to complain about?' But that's not how it works. If you're not in a team environment, you won't understand that a lot of what we do is a question of habit and feeling comfortable. You want to feel good with your surroundings. When lots of little things start changing it's destabilising. It doesn't matter if you are a footballer or working behind a machine in a factory: when you feel good in your working environment you tend to work better. You're more relaxed. In the end the product is better.

A much bigger problem was his approach to tactics. Moyes obviously wanted us to change our style … but we were never quite sure what he wanted to change it to.

While we were on our pre-season Asian tour he told me and a couple of others that he wanted us to play a narrow 4–2–2–2 with the wide players coming inside. I remember thinking: 'Have you not read up on this club's history? This club was *built* on wingers! It only goes back about 100 years! Cristiano Ronaldo, David Beckham, Ryan Giggs, Steve Coppell, Willie Morgan, George Best, David Pegg, Charlie Mitten, Billy Meredith … That's quite a long tradition there!' More to the point, what he was saying went totally against what any of the players here were used to. Playing 4–2–2–2 would mean revamping a big chunk of the squad which was built around wingers who were not the best at coming inside. We didn't play well in the pre-season games, but we never really play well pre-season. Our form usually kicks in around Christmas and January so I'll give him the benefit of the doubt. I want him to do well because that means I'll do well and we'll have more success.

But somehow his innovations mostly led to negativity and confusion. Under Fergie, for example, before a game on a Saturday we always played a small-sided match on a small pitch on the Friday. We loved it. We'd get into the mood for the following day by expressing ourselves, having fun, trying stuff out. You got your touch right, experimented, got the feeling flowing. We'd done that for years and suddenly – again for no good reason – Moyes changed it by making us play two-touch. There wasn't a strategy behind it; or, if there was, he never explained it to us well enough. Instead of enjoying these games, you'd hear the attackers moaning: 'I hate this fucking two-touch ...' It went against the grain of how we played. It was especially bad for the forwards who liked to practise their skills and shots and movements; they felt restricted. It didn't even have much to do with the way Moyes tried to get us to play. Even *I* was moaning about it and I'm a defender: you'd come off the pitch feeling blocked, frustrated, like you hadn't had a chance to express yourself. We complained, but nothing changed. Then people wondered why we looked cramped and played without personality or imagination.

There was also the business of preparing to defend set pieces. It wasn't something we'd ever spent much time on before. Fergie's approach was always to focus on the other team's weaknesses. We expected to win every game and he'd say things like 'They're rubbish in this area ... this is how we're going to destroy them.' For years we were one of the best teams at not conceding goals from corners and free

THE NICE GUY

kicks. Very occasionally, if a team had a special play, we'd do something on that. With Rory Delap's long throw-ins at Stoke, for example, Fergie would set us up and ask us, 'Are you comfortable with this?' Usually I'd mark Peter Crouch and leave Vida free to attack the ball. Or, if it went over Vida, I'd come and attack it. Just simple little things like that. For most games Fergie would leave the defending to us. We had it *down*: our method was simple, effective and something we always felt very secure about.

Yet with Moyes it was always how to stop the other side, and he was worried about other teams' corners and free kicks. Before every game, he made a point of showing us videos of how dangerous the other team could be. On the morning of a game we'd spend half an hour on the training ground drilling to stop them. But our defensive record definitely did not improve. There was so much attention to the subject it suddenly became a worry: they must be fucking good at this, to have us spend all this time on it …

That was the different mentality: Moyes set us up not to lose whereas we'd been accustomed to playing to win every game. Apart from 'Don't lose' I never thought Moyes had a philosophy he 100 per cent believed in and said 'Right, this is how we're going to play.' Did he want to carry on with Fergie's style or teach us his own style? Would we use wingers or keep things tight and play percentages? We never knew. I don't even think he knew or, if he did, he never communicated it to us well enough.

The biggest confusion was over how he wanted us to move the ball forward. Often he told us to play it long. Some players felt they kicked the ball long more than at any time in their career. Sometimes our main tactic was the long, high, diagonal cross. It was embarrassing. In one home game against Fulham we had 81 crosses! I was thinking: why are we doing this? Andy Carroll doesn't actually play for us! The whole approach was alien and we didn't even win the game.

Other times Moyes wanted lots of passing. He'd say: 'Today I want us to have 600 passes in the game. Last week it was only 400.' Who fucking cares? I'd rather score five goals from ten passes! There came a point where I was thinking: 'Do you actually want us to win, because if you're going to keep changing things it's obviously going to reduce your chances of winning.'

Why was he trying to change us anyway? We can't be too bad: we won the league by 11 points a few months ago! If I were you, I'd just get a couple of trophies under my belt first before trying to change everything. That would make a bit more sense.

At the beginning of the season Moyes told me: 'I want to go for experienced players.' After about eight games, we weren't playing particularly well, he said: 'OK, I'm going to have a look at the youngsters.' That's fair enough. If I was a young player, I'd want old guys out of the team as quick as possible too. But he overdid it. I suddenly went from being one of the best centre-backs in the league to not even travelling with the team and all the defenders were confused. A lot was made up about Moyes using Jagielka as an example to me and other defenders, but that never happened at all!

THE NICE GUY

'If you're under any sort of pressure I want you to make sure you've always got that ball out to the side,' he told us. 'I don't want you to take any risks.'

He was bringing the mentality of a smaller club. I never had the feeling Moyes knew how to speak like a Man United manager. You'd pick up the paper and see him saying unbelievable things like we 'aspire' to be like Man City or Liverpool were 'favourites' against us. If you want to survive, he's right: don't take risks. But this wasn't Everton; it was Man United. We don't want to *survive*. We want to *win*. Of course, when you're in your own box, you don't take risks. But when you're on the halfway line or in the opponents' half risks do need to be taken sometimes, especially tight, high-level games, if you're going to win.

It was as if he had no confidence in our abilities. Generally, with all due respect, the players at Man United are at a higher level than those at Everton. But we had the feeling he didn't trust us to execute things on the field. Even for me the feeling was: he doesn't trust me, he doesn't believe in me. No wonder players weren't going out and producing.

The mixed messages were even worse. Sometimes he'd say, 'I want you to pass the ball,' other days it was: 'I don't want you to pass the ball.' What the fuck do you want us to do, man? In the pool you heard a lot of guys complaining: 'I just don't know what he wants.' He had me doubting everything. Remember, we're all professionals so want to do what our manager is asking us to do; we want to please him; we want him to take us on and make us champions again. Whatever he says, we'll do.

In September, after Man City beat us 4–1 he called me and Vida into a meeting with the video analysis guy. 'I want to show you a few things,' said the manager. He had about 15 clips to show us, but we never got past clip five. We talked for about 40 minutes and came out none the wiser. It got pretty heated and I had the feeling he just wanted to cut the whole meeting short because he didn't like confrontation. That was another difference: Fergie would dig out anyone if he felt it would improve the team – but bad feeling would never be allowed to fester.

Ostensibly the idea for the video clips meeting was to understand what had gone wrong for City's goals. In one instance Moyes said: 'You could have done better here, you could have been tighter on Aguero …' And I said: 'OK, but Aguero is one of the quickest in the league and in the build-up there wasn't enough pressure on their midfield.' My point was that, if they've got players good enough to put the ball anywhere they want, going ultra-tight on Aguero was asking for trouble. The ball would just be played behind me and Aguero would be clean through. It would be better to hope the ball will be played to Aguero's feet. That way I can at least get tight behind him and stop him turning. But Moyes wouldn't answer the point. He kept saying: 'Yeah, but you should have been tighter.'

We held our hands up. 'Yes, OK,' I said 'there were points in the game where we could have defended better,' but we were trying to say it wasn't just a problem with the defence. Vida and I were getting opened up because the shape wasn't right; the whole team wasn't defending correctly. For their

THE NICE GUY

first goal, I'd headed the ball out but it had come back at us too easily; no one had put pressure on Matija Nastasić, Samir Nasri or Aleksanda Kolarov earlier in the move. I was trying to say that the best way to defend is to stop attacks at source or, failing that, to get into a good solid shape. We used to be so strong at that. But we weren't on the same page at all.

At one point I said: 'Look, if you want me to go tight, I'll go tight. That's the easiest thing for me to do as a defender. If that's what you want me to do, I'll do that. Just tell me!' And he was like: 'Yes, but I also want you to …' It was so confusing! Maybe he had a good point, but he never got it across. Me and Vida came out of there and looked at each other. 'I don't know what the fuck he just asked us to do,' I said to my teammate.

We just wanted clear and concise information, but everything was mixed. Some days it was 'Yeah, let's play wingers.' Did we think he believed it? No. Did we think he believed that he wanted us to pass the ball out from the back? No.

He'd tell me to come out with the ball – but kick it diagonal if there's nothing on. To my way of thinking, if there's nothing on, that probably means there's a problem in the team. Are we set up right? Is the movement good enough? Yes, of course there are times you have to belt the ball away. But if you're trying to create a pattern of play that shouldn't be your first thought. So I'm coming out with the ball and have no one to pass to. What am I supposed to do? Kick it long? Produce an unbelievable bit of magic as a centre-half? Sometimes I'd be about to pass the ball and think does he actually want me to pass the ball here? I doubted everything.

Was that what he wanted? I'd pass the ball and think *was that OK?* I'd take up position on the pitch and worry about it. Eventually in some games we'd just switch to autopilot and play the way we know from the old times.

Of course, there were aspects of his approach that impressed me. One of Moyes's first statements when he arrived was that he was going to focus on getting us to work harder, physically. 'I'm going to get you fitter,' he told the squad, 'I'm going to get you running harder.' He definitely stepped up the volume and intensity of training. He was enthusiastic; his work ethic was great. You could see how much he wanted to be a success at United. We had some good training sessions, and he was always present. Where Fergie usually left the training to people like Brian Kidd, Carlos Queiroz or Rene Meulensteen, Moyes was much more hands-on.

But another thing he told us very early went on to cause a lot of trouble. He said his method was to announce the team on the Friday or the Saturday before the game – and refuse to talk about it. If we weren't happy about being left out, then tough. He wasn't going to put an arm round your shoulder and he wouldn't be giving explanations. He said: 'If you've got something to say, come and see me Monday.' In other words, long after the game. That was a huge break away from Fergie's way of doing things.

Again, I thought: 'I'm sure that worked fine at Everton but things are different here.' At Everton you've only probably got 13 players in the squad who believe they should be playing every week, based on their ability. Most of the others in the squad are

THE NICE GUY

either young players or players happy to be on the bench. That's no disrespect to Everton; it was like that at West Ham when I was a kid. That's how it works at clubs just below the very top. But at Manchester United you've got 22 to 25 internationals who have won titles and cups and they all believe they should start. Common sense should tell you you've got to treat that workforce differently. Everton play 40 or 50 games a season, and only a few of those are high-intensity games against top teams. United play more like 60 games a season and a lot of those are big, must-win games. So a part of the art of being Manchester United manager is to rotate your squad and keep everyone happy.

Fergie was brilliant at that. He managed to keep the whole squad feeling involved. Take Chicharito [Javier Hernández]: he's a terrific player and his goal scoring record guarantees 15 to 20 goals a season. But Ferguson didn't actually start him in too many games; he preferred to use him as an impact player who'd win or rescue games at places like Stoke or Aston Villa. Javier did that a lot and he was happy for three years. All of a sudden, Moyes starts treating him differently and Chicarito's confidence goes. You could see the way he carried himself changed.

You have to respect and appreciate the fact that players have egos, and attacking players are the ones with the bigger egos. You need to give players the arm around the shoulder. Players live to play and we feel disappointed and hurt if we're not picked. Fergie would say: 'I'm not picking you this week because I'm saving you for next week.' The psychology was so clever: 'I'll give you a rest and give someone else a little chance, because I have to rotate the squad. But don't you worry. You get yourself ready, son. You get yourself ready for next week.' You forget about the game he's dropped you for and focus on next week.

Fergie was human about it; he was clever. He'd say: 'This is difficult for me, I don't enjoy doing this.' Sometimes you'd think: nah, that's bollocks I don't care what you're saying. One time he dropped me for a Liverpool game because we had Chelsea coming up. I was like: 'Not playing at Liverpool? But that's one of the biggest games of the season!' And he goes: 'I can't risk it because we have a Champions League game coming up.' At first, I was just angry. Then I thought: 'Yeah, but he still respects me as a footballer; he still believes I can play at one of the top teams, so he can't not like me anymore.' Then I'd be alright about it.

Most of the problems with Moyes seemed to come together for the match that effectively ended our season: the second leg of our Champions League quarter-final with Bayern Munich. In the previous round against Olympiacos we'd pulled off a great escape. In the first leg we were awful and lost 2–0, but in the return game at Old Trafford we turned it around and won 3–0.

By the time we went to Munich we had no chance of finishing in the top four of the Premier League and this was the last competition we could win. In the first game we'd drawn 1–1 and on the balance of chances really should have won. For almost the first time in the season our tactics were clear: Bayern were reigning champions and were still

THE NICE GUY

considered the best team in Europe so we played compact and looked to counter. For once Moyes gave us clear instructions: when I won the ball, I was going to look to play the ball behind their defenders. It was the first time I felt the whole team understood what the manager wanted. But even then he made a mistake playing Giggsy as a left-winger. Giggsy was 40 years old; how was he supposed to play left wing against a fullback bombing on all the time? He found it pretty taxing. But, as I say, things didn't go too badly. A week later came the game that was our last chance to save the season, maybe even David Moyes's job.

I was desperate to play, especially in that great stadium. And because I'd played well in the first game then didn't play against Newcastle, when I travelled to Munich I knew I must be in the team. On the morning of the game everything seemed wrong. To practise our set pieces and stuff we went to a public park. It was bizarre! Local people started coming from all over to watch us, take photos and videos. It's not how Manchester United do things! You don't want to be giving away the secrets of your formation and how you're going to play! I mean, why not just send Bayern an email or a DVD? It was amateurish.

But worse was to come. As we're standing there in public on this bit of grass, the manager just taps me on the shoulder and says: 'Rio, listen, I'm not going to play you. I feel we need a bit more pace in the back line.'

It killed me. Inside I wanted to scream and grab him. I'm a team player, so I just had to bite my tongue and stand there. But it was probably the worst single moment I ever had at

United. I'd never been dropped for a big a game like that, and to drop that on me in front of everybody when I can't react. 'Fucking hell; why didn't you tell me before?'

Objectively I just thought he was dead wrong. Chris Smalling, who was going to play in my place, had been injured. The Bayern strikers, Thomas Müller and Mario Mandžukić, weren't blisteringly quick; pace wasn't their game; it didn't make any sense. I'd rather he just said, 'I think Chris Smalling is in better form than you are,' or something like that. But it was just the way he told me. I didn't even get a chance to say my piece. He might not want to hear it, but it just leaves you feeling frustrated. He must have known 24 hours beforehand that I wasn't going to play. If he'd told me earlier I could have dealt with it better.

Several teammates told me later that my reaction was something they'd never seen from me before. I went into a daze and even took my anger and the debate about him onto the coach as we waited for him to finish doing set pieces with the first XI. I'd never shown my feelings like that in front of my teammates so openly before. My anger came out straight away with no filter. I knew my time at United was coming to an end and, where I had once had time to prove myself, I felt this was different.

Not being involved in the game, at least I had the chance to watch how it all went wrong. Sir Alex used to give simple, concise, clear instructions. Depending on the opponents, he'd say: 'Tight early on,' or 'Blow them away early.' The thing he always stressed was: CONCENTRATE! That was his favourite. But before the game Moyes said that, depending

THE NICE GUY

how Bayern played, we could use three different formations! He'd let the lads know which one when the game got underway. Danny Welbeck was going to play on the right ... or it could be on the left ... or behind. Shinji Kagawa was definitely going to play behind, or the left ... all through the team. The whole thing created uncertainty: how could Danny prepare if he had to think about doing four different jobs on the pitch? It even puts doubt in the mind of experienced players. Wayne Rooney would normally be sitting in the dressing room before a game thinking: 'Right, I know that I'm centre-half, so I'll make these kind of runs, and if he comes tight I'll spin him.' We all try to see the game in our minds before we play. Of course players have to be able to adapt but people were going onto the pitch not knowing what they were supposed to do.

In the event, the team played much the same way we started, defending and looking for a quick break. It almost worked: Patrice Evra scored a fantastic goal out of nothing and for a few minutes it looked like we could get through. Then Bayern scored three quick goals and it was all over. What was fascinating was watching Moyes in action. Or in *inaction*. Fergie's approach was always the same: we're going to beat everyone. I noticed the difference between the two benches – ours was animated and nervous with Moyes moaning about every decision; Pep Guardiola, on the other hand, was completely calm. One of the things a great manager does is create a mentality throughout the club. Like Diego Simeone at Atlético Madrid: he makes everyone feel involved. It's not just the players who determine results; it's the players who aren't playing, and the backroom staff – from the kit man to the sports scientists. The staff have to be happy; it's part of what keeps players going sometimes. As I understand it, Moyes actually did that at Everton. But he couldn't do it at Manchester United. At Everton the objective wasn't: 'Let's win every game and every trophy.' It was: 'Let's not get beaten by Manchester United and the other top four teams.' By the time he left us I don't think a lot of the staff even really felt part of his team.

Well, as everyone knows, the Bayern game turned out to be one of his last games in charge. Eleven days later he took the team to Everton – I didn't travel – and we got thumped 2–0. Two days later he was sacked. It wasn't done in a dignified way: the club let rumours circulate for almost two days before putting him out of his misery. But, as you'd expect, David Moyes behaved with great dignity.

Us players were as much in the dark as the fans. The club never told us a thing. I only found out Moyes had gone when Anders Lindegaard texted us all to say 'It's official, guys. It's official.' I drove to the training ground at Carrington as normal; outside there were dozens of TV cameras. Inside, a players' meeting had been called. Everyone knew why.

Moyes came in with Steve Round and Jimmy Lumsden and said they were all leaving. He didn't sound happy with the way information had leaked out the day before, and we could understand that. We've all got our pride and our families, after all.

He made a good speech: 'I've had a fantastic time here

THE NICE GUY

but unfortunately we've not had the results, and it's a results driven game, so … um … I've been sacked. This is the best club in the world, make sure you try and stay here as long as you can. And all of us, I am sure, our paths will cross again in the future.'

He thanked us again, said goodbye and shook everyone's hands, and that was it. Then Giggsy came in, and made a little speech saying he was manager till the end of the season. When he was finished, I had a question for him. I said: 'What do we call you? Gaffer? Giggsy? What?' And he laughed and said 'Giggsy' was fine. Then we went out and straight into the day's training.

It's an unforgiving game. Obviously you feel sad for somebody who loses their job, but as a professional all you can do is get on with things and move on. It's a bit cold, but that's the business that we're in. Things change fast in football; the next game against Norwich was coming up and you just have to put everything else out of your mind. I didn't know something similar would happen to me a few weeks later. But it was the only way to react. You know a career can be over very suddenly; it's something everyone at some point has to go through. You've just got to get on with things and keep moving on.

Some people argue the manager is overrated in modern football. But one of the things the whole saga showed me was just how important the manager can be in a club. Even if you've got great and highly motivated players it all has to be channelled in the right way; you need someone to put all the elements together. Someone's got to create the right environment in the changing room; someone's got to create an environment that carries out onto that pitch. It doesn't just happen by itself. You can't just throw a group of players together and expect them to be a great team – someone at the top has to be driving that.

You can see the difference between the confusing Moyes approach and the absolute clarity Louis van Gaal brought to the job. I'm just disappointed I didn't get a chance to work with him because it would have been an education. The players at United now tell me Van Gaal is strong and determined and clear in his methods and his philosophy. If you can't buy into his philosophy, he'll find players who can. There was a fascinating quote from him: 'I am training the players not in their legs but in their brain, in brain power.' I think I could have learned a lot from Van Gaal.

Looking back, I'd say David Moyes was unlucky. He and Manchester United were just oil and water somehow. His ideas weren't bad in themselves; they just didn't fit with the group of players and the tradition and recent history of the club. As players we also have to stand up and be counted and say we didn't perform. It's a fact. But at the same time we needed to be given the right framework and structure for our strengths to come out. We get paid to play well, and the fact that we failed wasn't for lack of effort. We tried as hard as we could. But we didn't play to our strengths under Moyes.

It was always going to be hard for him following such a huge character not just at the club but in the world of football. Don't forget he also had the added disadvantage of arriving

THE NICE GUY

just after the departure of David Gill, the chief executive who was very influential in buying players and running the club. United was in transition and it would've been difficult for any new manager. Even so, David Moyes wasn't right for Man Utd – he wasn't clear in his ideas and he couldn't get what he wanted over to the players.

The question of who was to blame does keep going back and forth in my mind, though. I wish he could have seen me last season, when I had one of my best seasons at United, or a few years ago when I was fighting fit and in my prime. I don't think I was responsible for him getting sacked. I couldn't have given more, but I do wish I could have played consistently well under him. He might have been still in the job, or at least he'd have seen me in a better light as a player. On the other side, you think: 'Did he set us up properly to be able to give the best of ourselves as players?' No, he didn't. But that's the kind of tennis game you have in your head: 'Was it me? … Was it him? …' That's what goes round in your mind if you're a good professional. You never say: 'Oh it's *his* fault.' You are always at odds with yourself a bit. Was it him or was it me? It's a never-ending rally.

On Pressure and Boredom

It does strange things to you

Some players just don't cope with the pressure of being in the England squad. Like Jimmy Bullard. Jimmy might never have set the world alight for England – but he was a hell of a good player I knew from way back. He made two squads but never actually got a game. It was a shame. And I think it tells us something about another thing that is wrong with England.

I knew Jimmy when we were about 11 and played against each other in the Bexley and Kent League. He was with YMCA and I played for Eltham Town. He was one of the most sought-after young players in the area – technically good, very fit. He could shoot and pass, and he was built like a marathon runner. Then I lost track of him and I heard he went into painting and decorating. Then years later, he turned up at the West Ham reserves, then went off and did well for himself. He became bit of a cult figure along the way at places like Wigan, Fulham and Hull. I think fans saw themselves in him: he was a kind of 'Jack the Lad' mess-about-merchant who never took himself too seriously. But he was always a better footballer than most people noticed.

When Jimmy retired he wrote a very funny book, pointing out, among other things, that Fabio Capello looks just like *Postman Pat*. He also made a serious point about the oppressive seriousness of the England setup. He felt a bit lost within the system, was never comfortable and couldn't flourish. I've spoken to him about it and it was a real problem. He said the seriousness of the England camp just made it impossible for him to be himself so he didn't really train that well.

It's an issue because you go away and you're suddenly completely outside your comfort zones. Like with food. At home you eat when you want. Normally I eat with my kids at about 6pm and if I feel like having something else later, I'll just go to the fridge. But with the national team everything is so regimented. It's almost like being in prison!

I remember one time we played a game on the Wednesday and had another game on Saturday. That left us locked in the hotel for days. So after the Wednesday match John Terry, Ashley Cole, Shaun Wright-Phillips and I organised to get some Nando's in for all the lads. We knew they'd be hungry and wouldn't want the official food. So we all went to dinner with the team, but ate minimally, knowing the Nandos was on its way. After half an hour we left the dinner table and … enjoyed the food we wanted. If you could've heard us! We were like hyenas at feeding time with a limitless supply of dead wildebeest. If somebody had got those sound effects on tape it would've been hilarious.

ON PRESSURE AND BOREDOM

We did that sort of thing a couple of times. Another time we went for McDonald's and everyone ordered Big Macs, and chicken burgers and stuff. It was quite an operation: the food would be delivered through the back of the hotel by one of the lads' drivers. In the normal run of things you'd never think of doing that; it would only ever be once in a blue moon. We're not stupid. We know what to eat. But we were stir-crazy: we'd been locked away for like a week and no one had had any food they really enjoyed. At times like that that kind of stuff tastes fantastic. It's a reaction to being bossed about.

One time Fabio Capello said we couldn't have butter on our toast in the morning. I remember sitting there and putting olive oil and salt on instead. What would be worse? The olive oil and salt, I'm sure. Or another time it would be: 'no ice cream'. We were absolutely forbidden to have even a tiny bit of ice cream. I mean – we're only with the team for about *four or five days*. Do you really think it's going to affect my performance if I put a bit of butter on my toast when that's what I do every other day of the year?

Sometimes you have to give players responsibility. We're all professionals; we didn't get to this point in our lives by being unprofessional. We can look after ourselves. If you treat us like kids we'll behave like kids.

It's not just food. I remember in Glenn Hoddle's time – because he was as strict as anyone else in this regard – we were at the hotel in Burnham Beeches and we weren't allowed out anywhere. I was 19 or 20 years old and used to going out all the time. Suddenly I was in what felt like

151

a prison lockdown. So I asked one of my mates to come and get me in his car after dinner. The routine was that we would finish training and then have lunch at 1.30pm or 2pm … and then there was nothing to do until a 7.30pm meeting! So we were supposed to sit in the hotel the whole time. It freaked me out. So I'd get my mates to wait with the car outside, by the perimeter wall. I'd sneak through the kitchens, escape through the back door then jump over the back wall. Me and Frank Lampard did that a couple of times: all we wanted was to go for a drive or to the local town listening to music and chilling – just normal 18- or 19-year-old stuff but without the alcohol. We never drank. And we were never the worse for it, I can assure you. It wasn't like being off clubbing – we just didn't want to be stuck in the room. You'd never do that at home, so why do it before a big game? You just seize up. Boredom is a problem.

Long, boring stays in hotels can have a dark side as well. Being stuck away from home, alone in a room, players can easily get caught up in gambling. It's just a laugh at first, but within a couple of months you can easily find yourself chasing hundreds of thousands of pounds. At that point you are too deep in a hole to climb out, and you can't speak to anyone because you're either embarrassed or genuinely addicted.

I talk from experience. I was once £200,000 down because I was gambling on rugby, dogs and horses. I gambled by text and on credit and the process was so easy I was in trouble almost before I realised. My bookie knew I was good for the money, and I started with bets of a couple of grand here and there. Next thing I know, I owe him £200,000 and I'm worried sick.

In the end, I was very lucky to escape. I managed to get my debt down to £107,000, then staked the whole amount on an evens bet on the favourite in a seven horse race. Watching on TV that horse seemed to run in slow motion and I was panicking. But after some of the scariest minutes of my life, it came in and I was able to settle my debt. But I'd learned my lesson. I paid the bookie what I owed – then told him never to send me odds or contact me again and deleted him from my phone.

Roy Keane

Is he putting this on?

I have say that as a captain Roy Keane was brilliant in most departments. He'd run the training and be very disciplined about it. If people seemed to be taking their foot off the pedal he would hammer them. He called a meeting once to have a go at Darren Fletcher for talking on his phone, and laid into some of the other young lads for not going to the gym and doing extra training. That was all good because the younger lads started to change their ways – and that was needed. But the next day I walked in and saw Roy talking on his phone, doing the exact same thing he had criticised Fletcher for! I just raised my eyebrows to say 'Woah, you remember what you said yesterday?' He just kind of smiled in embarrassment. He was probably thinking: 'Yeah, but I can do this because I'm a senior player – I've worn the T-shirt, I was talking to the younger lads.'

The only thing that I was really gutted about was that I didn't get to play with Roy during his best years. He was still a top player when I arrived; he knew the game and dictated a lot of matches by the way he played, but he wasn't at the peak of his powers.

In his book Ferguson says how great Roy was as a player then says he could be very harsh with people: 'The hardest part of Roy's body is his tongue ...' It's true that in the changing room he would come down on people, especially on Ollie, John O'Shea and Fletcher. With those three I think he saw a little bit of himself, especially Sheasy and Fletcher. They were young lads who came over from another country and he didn't want to see them coasting or resting on their laurels.

I remember one player, Michael Stewart, a young Scottish midfielder who was talented and the club had high hopes for him. After training one day, Michael was taking off his boots and Keane went over to him and said 'I can see you're going to be one of those players who, in a couple years, will be at Accrington Stanley or some non-league team, telling your teammates how you used to share a changing room with guys like Roy Keane and Ruud van Nistelrooy rather than being out there playing with us.' And the kid – you could see it – he was broken. But he went on to play for Scotland and had a good career in the Scottish Premier League.

Yes, Roy could be very cutting. I remember he said something to me after we lost 2–0 to Liverpool in the League Cup Final. He was shouting at everyone and he turned on me: '30 fucking million? Well, you ain't proved nothing yet.' I sat there thinking, why is he digging me out? I said something back like: 'Yeah, you can fucking talk, you just keep talking.'

But he just kept shouting at the lads: 'How can we fucking lose to people like Liverpool?'

I wasn't one to worry about stuff like that. I don't mind confrontation in the changing room – I think it's better than not saying anything. If you can't deal with it then get out. When I was growing up me and my brothers were shouting at each other all the time. At West Ham there were fights on the training ground; Leeds, though, had a young squad when I was there, and there wasn't so much volatility.

When I went to Man United it was so much more intense. People were fighting and clashing all the time. Ronaldo and Ruud van Nistelrooy practically came to blows because Ronaldo wouldn't cross the ball. It was around that time when Ruud was really frustrated because we were in a transitional period and we hadn't won anything for a couple of years. He even took a swing at me once. But that's how much the game meant to him. Ruud and I got on really well but this was just one of those times when he saw red. He had kicked Ronaldo on the floor in training because his frustration was boiling over, and then I kicked him. Next time the ball came into him I went down the back of his achilles a little bit and he turned and tried to swing at me. I leaned back out of the way and said: 'Swing at me like that, make sure you fucking hit me next time.' Then we got back in the changing room and all of a sudden he's gone. But that was the professionalism. Nothing was ever carried over; no one fell out for long and then we'd be laughing about it.

But Keane could lose it. Even meeting with the manager he'd be quite confident. He said: 'I don't care.' To be honest, the famous interview for Manchester United TV, where he criticised his teammates and which led to Ferguson kicking him out of the club, was quite mild for him. When I watched the video I thought, this is tamer than I'd heard him before. Nobody had seen him in public giving the lads an ear-bashing. At the same time, like the manager, I thought if you've got something to say your teammates, as a captain, as a professional, I don't think doing it in the press, in the media, is the right way to do it. If the manager wants to do it, it's up to him; it's his prerogative. If you're one of the team, whether you're captain or not, I don't think it's your job to do that. But Roy was adamant. He said 'I'd say this to anyone. I'd do it again ...'

When he left you could see Fletcher, O'Shea and Wes Brown's personality came out more. It was almost like they were able to breathe a little bit. They flourished and grew. We went on to be very successful and those three guys were an important part of that.

When Roy left Manchester United he was seen as having a 'dark side' to his character, but when he started appearing on TV everyone saw he has a good, dry sense of humour too. The frustrating thing was that you couldn't read him. I used to think to myself: is he acting? He'd come in with a face of thunder and you'd think, fucking hell, I think he's going to blow up on someone soon today. But most of the time, he was involved in jokes, messing about. We had a really good, funny changing room then and he was involved in most of the jokes. If anyone was to be laughed at, or anyone was wearing bad gear, he would bring them down straightaway. Roy could take it as well. He always used to cane people for doing photo shoots or anything like that. He'd say, 'you're a footballer – what's wrong with you?' On one occasion someone brought in a magazine that featured Roy doing adverts for 'Diadora' or 'Seven-Up', and Giggs absolutely ripped into him and he just kind of laughed it off.

I was surprised when he went on TV as a pundit because I remember him seeing old players on screen and the amount of abuse he used to give them! He even muted the TV so you couldn't hear them. I used to think: 'When he retires from football nobody is ever going to see this guy.' But then he started appearing on TV every other week and he showed people a different side to his character.

So he wasn't 'Mr. Unhappy' all the time, just a little bit of an unstable personality, a bit 'Jekyll and Hyde.' Every now and again he would erupt over something really trivial. And you wouldn't be able to read him. Sometimes I thought: Is he putting this on? I could never quite work him out.

Roy could be absolutely brilliant. I remember the famous game against Arsenal at Highbury. After the warm-up before the game Patrick Vieira punched Gary Neville on his way off the pitch. In the changing room Gary said: 'Fucking hell, he just punched me,' and all lads turned round. What you talking about?

'Fucking Vieira just punched me in my back after the warm-up.'

The lads were already up. We thought: he ain't getting away with punching one of our players! Roy said nothing. But as we're standing in the tunnel, out of nowhere, he just explodes and goes crazy at Vieira and the TV cameras caught it all. That's all folklore now but look at the psychology: there was no way we were going to lose that game after that. We won 4–2. That was the good element of his captaincy – Roy took responsibility full on.

Black Coaches

We can be the generation of change

Almost half the talent in the Premier League is made up of black or mixed-race players. For there to be no representation of this at executive level and among coaches makes no sense. Why don't we have more black managers? Is it because of racism, as some people reckon? Or is there a more prosaic answer?

The question comes up when I'm talking to older black players or recently retired black players, I ask: 'Have you got your coaching badges yet?' 'Nah, no point man, I'm not going to get a job am I?' I understand the feeling because there are very few black managers to look to as an example. But I think it's a defeatist attitude. First, go and get your badges, then go for the job. Then, if you get turned down, you can start looking at the reasons why. If you've not got your badges and say 'I'm not going to get a job,' that's like saying: 'I want to play for that team because I'm great.' So are you going to try out for them? 'Nah, no point. The manager will never pick me.' How do you know if you've not tried?'

A lot of black players and players coming to the end of their careers do feel they'll be denied the opportunity to coach. But maybe the problem is different. Management and coaching tends to be a 'friend' business. If you're a mate of someone, you'll get a job. That's what often happens and sometimes it's not the best man who gets the job. The deciding factor is if you or your agent know a chairman. Have guys like Paul Ince and Chris Hughton suffered in their coaching career because they're black? Chris did an unbelievable job at Newcastle then went to Norwich, did a very good job, established them solidly in the Premier League and then, when they started struggling, got the sack. That was normal manager stuff. I don't think it would've made any difference what colour he was. I don't think if he were white he'd have got more time. Your team is doing badly – you're the scapegoat. I don't really know Chris, but he's a genuinely nice guy. He sent me a letter around that time of the stuff with my brother and John Terry and he's always going to have a job in football because he's a real football man and carries himself the right way. Why has Paul Ince had difficulties? I don't know. Maybe he just picked funny jobs. He certainly did well at MK Dons, but from there it was a bit of a rollercoaster. Chris Powell was doing well at Charlton and then all of a sudden things changed at that club. But was that because he's black? I don't think so.

But it is striking that previous generations of great black British football men like Ian Wright, John Barnes, Des Walker and Viv Anderson haven't made their mark as managers. John Barnes tried a bit at Celtic but he's never had a sniff since. That generation seems to have slipped past and, of course, once you leave the game for a couple of years, it's hard to get back in.

Nevertheless, I think change is in the air. Recently-retired players with obvious potential to be good managers such as Sol Campbell are now doing their badges. Hopefully my generation will be the generation that changes the picture. Hopefully we can start to break through and dispel any feeling that there is a glass ceiling for players of colour.

My Week and My Music

Play
Recover
Prepare
Play
Recover

Lots of people are curious about how players actually spend their days, so I'll just give you a rundown of how a typical week at Man United would go.

Monday

Let's say we've got a Champions League game at Old Trafford on the Wednesday, I'd start with my own hour-long routine in the gym: some stretching to maintain stability in my back, some loosening up exercises over hurdles and a bit of core work for the abdominals which support the back. That would take about an hour. And then I'll go out to training which would be a short, light, sharp training session. There wouldn't be any tactical work, just a short five-a-side type keep-ball game just to get everyone's legs moving for about an hour.

After that, I'd go back in the gym, and probably do some upper body work, again for my back: pull-ups, press-ups, dips. In the gym, I'd mostly be on my own, but maybe with one of the physios for the stretching stuff. One of the sports science team would always be in the gym anyway. Maybe I'd do a bit of yoga, too, depending how I feel.

Tuesday

The main event would be a really short field session with a bit more emphasis on tactics than the previous day. Then we'd do between 10 and 20 minutes working on their phases of play: how they move the ball from back to front. Do they work it through the lines? Do they work it as a long ball? Which of their players trigger certain movements. On the day of the game we'd be shown more detailed videos of which of their players we need to be more wary of, which areas do they like to play, that sort of stuff, but that would be backing up what we'd already done in the field. Sometimes it would be helpful. A situation would come up in the game and you'd think: 'Oh, I know what this is.' Every day after training – at least 90 per cent of the time – I have a sleep for about an hour or an hour and a half in the afternoon. When I get home I'll be spending most of my time thinking about the opponent I'll be playing against. How does he like to attack? I'll be thinking about details, but not too much. And I'll probably be thinking about the stuff I've seen in the videos. At home, food is very important: I'll eat well, load some carbohydrates, pasta and rice, wholemeal.

MY WEEK AND MY MUSIC

Wednesday

We wouldn't do anything too intense in training: just a little mini warm-up then and watch a video of the opposing team. That would focus on how they attack, a few bits on their danger man, how they concede goals, maybe some set pieces and that would be it, really. The coach would talk us through the video, pointing out little quirks of players: 'So and so is dominant left foot, he likes to shoot in such-and-such a way, he's got a quick trigger … ' that kind of thing. After that we head to the hotel where we have lunch, sleep, wake up, then have a pre-match meal about three hours before kickoff. The meal would be heavy carbohydrates, pasta. Well, mine is normally pasta. So: a big bowl of pasta, a plain piece of chicken with a little bit of mashed potato and maybe a couple of bread rolls. Then I'll have a yogurt with honey, and a banana, and then a cup of coffee.

Then we go to the stadium and prepare for the game.

Music has always been important for me. At United I made it an important part of our pre-match ritual as well. When I first started I liked really hard hip-hop but over the years I adapted the playlist to take account of the fact that different people had different musical tastes. There'd be older guys like the physios and Albert, the kit man, who didn't like hip hop. Fergie was always good-naturedly complaining: 'This isn't real music! Haven't you got any Sinatra?' But he was brilliant about it. His attitude was that if music was good for the team he was happy. So I created a mix of different genres for all tastes, from 'Fast Car' by Tracy Chapman, or Stone Roses's 'Fools Gold', which is my favourite song by the Manchester band, to more current stuff by people like Jay-Z and Drake. The way it worked was that we would get to the dressing room about an hour and a half before kick-off. First we'd have a meeting and after that everyone would start getting changed – and on goes the music. I'd put it on loud and the lads would be doing their pre-match routines: stretching, having massages, putting on strappings. The music would be on in the background, making everyone feel good, relaxing us. Of course, you'd get the odd person saying: 'this song is rubbish! Get it off!' so I'd move on to the next one! Over the years these were the playlist favourites:

- Right Before My Eyes (N'n'G feat. Kallaghan)
- Fast Car (Tracy Chapman)
- Fools Gold (The Stone Roses)
- Bartender (T-Pain, ft.Akon)
- Successful (Drake, ft. Lil Wayne)
- Sweet Child O' Mine (Guns N' Roses)
- Wonderwall (Oasis)
- Crazy Baldhead (Bob Marley)
- In Da Club (50 cent)
- P's & Q's (Kano)
- Beautiful Day (U2)
- A Milli (Lil Wayne)
- Little Bit of Luck (DJ Luck & Mc Neat)
- Started from the Bottom (Drake)
- Juicy (The Notorious B.I.G.)
- Dirt Off Your Shoulder (Jay-Z)
- Enough is Enough (Y-Tribe)

MY WEEK AND MY MUSIC

- Hold You (Gyptian)
- Niggas in Paris (Kanye West & Jay-Z)

I'd always have someone to play two-touch in the changing room. At one time it was Ronaldo, for four or five years it would be Scholesy. In my last season it would have been Adnan or Mata or sometimes Vidić. Just two-touch, keeping the ball up, three games of ten, normally. We'd just find a place in the changing room or in the hallway, depending on how big the changing room was if we were playing away. The idea, of course, is just to get a good feel of the ball. Sometimes I'd do it with bare feet, sometimes in socks, sometimes with my boots on. Scholesy was the best. If he was losing he'd just smash the ball at you so you couldn't get it back. Really it should be to feet and thighs only. But sometimes he would smash it so hard and low near the floor that it was almost impossible for you to get it back.

Then you go out and do the warm-up.

Then you play the game.

Then you don't sleep.

Or at least you don't sleep very much. After a game the adrenaline just keeps pumping through your body and you can't stop thinking about how the game went, especially if you've lost. You think about what you could have done differently, all the ifs, buts and maybes constantly running the game through your mind again and again. If you're lucky you might get to sleep about three or four o'clock in the morning. It doesn't matter if it's a big game or a small game. It just goes round and round and round in your mind.

Thursday

The next morning is mainly about recovering from the night before. You'll do a small run, then a warm-down session where you go on the bike for 20 minutes, then do a stretching routine on the mats. But that's just for the team that played last night. The lads who didn't play go out and do a full, normal training session. After the stretching you go to the pool and basically just float for half an hour. We call it 'deep floating', sitting in the water on a float. It flushes the lactic acid out of your muscles and loosens you up. Then you finish training with massages … and then home again.

Friday

There's a league game coming up tomorrow, so the team prepares for training with a 'quick feet' exercise to get us moving again and then we'd play a little match. Often this would be an old v. young versus game, which is usually a battering for the young lads. Then we'd go in and get ready for the game in much the same way as we had in midweek. Same balance of rest and work, same food, sleep, same tactical preparation with videos.

In my last three seasons at United, when I was more susceptible to injury, if I played on a Wednesday, then on the Friday, the second recovery day, while the lads went out for hard training, I'd join in the piggy-in-the-middle session before training, then just do some strides: running from box to box probably about eight times. And then take part in the match at the end. I'd limit myself to movement and make

MY WEEK AND MY MUSIC

sure I don't do anything too ballistic. There were claims in the media that Moyes over-trained us but I wouldn't say that.

For a Saturday game, whether we're playing home or away, we'd always go to a hotel. After training I'd have a couple of hours of sleep at home then I'd go to the hotel with the team. My Friday evening meal would be a bowl of pasta with a little bit of Bolognaise on top, then chicken or a little bit of steak maybe and – in Fergie's time – low-fat chips with vegetables like broccoli. Then I'd have a nice pudding, normally a little bit of sponge and ice-cream. In my room, just before I go to bed I'd usually have a chocolate bar or some chocolate biscuits.

Saturday

On match days, I wake up at about 7.30 or 8.00am, go down for breakfast straightaway and have either an omelette or a fried egg on toast, then a yogurt and probably a banana. That's all there for us on the buffet-type service at the hotels. Sometimes I have porridge instead of eggs. The pre-match meal is always three hours before kickoff. So, if the game starts at 3 o'clock, we eat at 12pm. If it's 5 o'clock, the meal is at 2pm. The tough ones are the games played early for TV. If we have to play at 1pm, say, we miss breakfast and just have the pre-match meal. It's disgusting to sit there and eat a big bowl of pasta at 10am. But you've got to force it down so that you've got the right food in your system to perform. (It's strange now to look back and remember that as an 18-year-old at West Ham my pre-match meal basically consisted of beans on toast, a bit of chicken, and maybe a banana and loads of water. Part of the reason I ate so little must have been down to nerves. I had so much nervous energy I wasn't hungry. The amount I eat now is huge compared to that!)

At United we developed a silly ritual of asking for coffees. There were four of us: me, Jonny Evans, Wayne Rooney and Giggsy, and one of us would go, 'Can I have a coffee?' And then the others would go, 'Yeah, me too, me too, me too' in sequence, like dominos falling. Sometimes there'd be other people at the table. It might be Paul Scholes, Robin van Persie, Vidić, Carrick, Fletcher. Whoever it was, I'd put my hand up and then we all would. And we'd all have our coffee. Then in the changing room, I'd go and have a Red Bull as well. It all adds to the adrenalin.

Then we do our normal pre-match stuff and then we play the game.

After the game we get given loads of goody bags, loads of chocolates and sweets because they want us to get a lot of sugar back in our systems immediately after the games. So, on the coach on the way home from the game or something, it's like a sweet shop, with sweets and chocolate and fizzy drinks and supplement drinks with loads of protein and carbohydrates in them which we have to drink straightaway in the changing room. On a Saturday night after a game I get insomnia. Win, lose, or draw I can be tweeting at three or four in the morning sometimes because I can't sleep. That's because the game is still ticking over in your mind and the adrenalin is still pumping through my system. The early kickoffs are easier sleep-wise because you've got whole day to wear off, but it's still difficult.

MY WEEK AND MY MUSIC

Sunday

The day after the game I'd go in for a warm down. Get on the bikes, go in pool to flash all the lactic acid and tightness out of your legs. I would normally do a gym session as well. Then I'd go home and play in the garden for a couple of hours with the kids, have a sleep and then a roast dinner. If the kids let me, I'll try and get on the sofa and watch the Sunday football.

And then the week starts again.

Trash Talkers

Get your legs on
You got no legs
Where's your legs?

Football is a psychological game so you're having individual duels with opponents all the time. You're trying to read them and dominate them. *What's the striker thinking?* He doesn't seem as quick as me; he's not as strong as me; he's not comfortable when I'm around him; I think he's scared of me. If I go up for a header and leave a bit on with an elbow, or I rub my studs down his back a little bit … I know players who, if I do that in the first couple of minutes, they won't come near me again. They'll look for somewhere else to play for the rest of the match. We're all looking for that edge. Strikers have their tricks; we have ours.

Sometimes the battle is verbal. I'm a fan of trash-talking, although it's not something I hear very often on the field. Maybe that's because, when I was playing for United we won most of the time and players who trash-talk and get beaten lose face. But it's one of the things I love about American sports. The interaction you get in basketball and NFL is just fantastic. I dream about that stuff. If I'd been a striker, you'd never have shut me up. I'd have been box office! I'd have been shouting from the rooftops. Before every game, I'd use social media and the papers to call out the centre-back I'd be facing in the next game. 'You've got no chance tomorrow. I'm going to destroy you …' And I'd keep it going in the game. I'd leave my defender for dead and get a shot off. Then I'd say: 'Do *not* let that happen again because I will punish you next time. Look at you! Get your legs on. You got no legs. Where's your legs?' I'd work on his confidence. First time he touches the ball: 'Ooh, you look nervous. The fans can see it too. They can see you're in bits. I'm worried for you. This just ain't the stage for you … this is too big for you.'

That's the way to do it. I might even put my arm round his shoulder. 'Listen, man, I'm here for you if you need me, yeah?' There's no point insulting the guy. 'You're a mug, you're a bastard' is water off a duck's back. 'I don't think you're really up to this level, man' is better. Or: 'I'm going to take it easy today. I'll still destroy you, but I won't go full pelt because I feel sorry for you. I don't want to end your career.' Next time he touches the ball he'll be a nervous wreck.

Sadly, I could never get involved in that sort of thing because I'm a defender. As a defender it's just asking for trouble. Let's say for 90 minutes my striker hasn't touched the ball; I've bullied him all game – he's got no chance. I'm quicker than him, smarter than him and even if he does bring the ball down, turn and face me, I'll take it off him. Then, in injury time, he gets a lucky deflection and the ball ends up in the back of the net! If I've been trash-talking him all game, he can turn round and absolutely open me up. It's like when I played against Fernando Torres. Usually he didn't get a sniff. But once in a while he did OK. And what happened? People said: 'Torres ripped you apart in that game.' You think to yourself, 'Well, I've played against the geezer about eight times now and he ain't touched the ball in five or six of them.' But that's the life of a defender.

Different players have different ways of trying to unsettle you. When I was 18, I played against Ian Wright, who'd been a hero of mine when I was growing up. The ball was down the other end because we had a corner, so I was standing on the halfway line, marking him. He was kind of staring at me. Then he starts pointing at my head. He's going: 'Look at you, look at you. You skinny this and that, you think you're fucking good, don't ya?' and he's trying to touch my head. As I move his hand away, he goes 'Yeah, I've got you! I'm inside your head now. I'm *inside* there.' I thought: 'cheeky bastard'. I hated him. But after the game he comes up all friendly and joking and goes 'no, no, that's only on the pitch, blah, blah' I was like: 'I don't like this guy.' Though I grew to be friends with him later.

Craig Bellamy had a style all his own. He used to trash-talk his own teammates. He'd say things like: 'Look at him! What's he doing on this pitch? He's rubbish! ... Look what I'm having to play with! ... How the hell am I having to play with this crap?' It wouldn't be fair to tell you the names of the people he mentioned. I never knew if he was doing it seriously or was just trying to get a percentage on me. But he was hilarious.

Occasionally you get people who just get it completely wrong – like Danny Shittu at Watford. It was the first day of the season, Watford's first day back in the Premier League, and he was in the tunnel making noise. He might just have been plain nervous, but lots of teams promoted from the Championship do that. They think shouting makes them sound big. But we were a quiet team. We preferred to go out and let our football do the talking. Anyway, Danny hadn't quite got the hang of the intimidation thing because what he was shouting was: 'Come on boys! They're only human.' We were all looking at each other as if to say: 'What was *that*? Is he joking?' We just smelt fear when we heard that. You've got to be shouting the right stuff, man!

To be fair, Watford played well. I think we won 2–1, but it was a tight game. It was often hard to play against newly promoted teams in the first weeks of the season. When the new fixtures come out, the first games I look for are always Liverpool, Man City, West Ham – because they're my old club – and then the newly promoted teams. You want to avoid them early in the season. You'd rather play them after ten games or so, when their adrenaline's gone. Newly promoted teams often cause a few upsets early in the season because they're high on being in the top league.

And so, of course, are their supporters. Then again, noisy crowds never bothered me. We played at Galatasaray and Besiktas in Istanbul and those grounds were so loud before kickoff it was just bananas. But at the same time, you don't hear what the crowd is saying. Anfield is noisy but you don't really hear what's going on. Celtic is probably the loudest I've

TRASH TALKERS

heard. The roar there before a Champions League game was unbelievable. I know the fans at these places were trying to intimidate us, but I always found it a turn-on. The hairs on the back of your neck stand up and you look at your teammates and say 'Yes! This is why we play football!' Then you go out and go straight into it. I love the passion and intensity. The more fans against us, the more satisfying it is when you win. So it's an incentive.

What bothered me was silence. I always found the hardest players were the ones you couldn't read – the ones who showed no emotion. People like Bergkamp, Raul, Messi, Xavi, Iniesta, and Zidane weren't just incredible technicians, they were deadpan. You could stare at them; you could try and nudge them; you could shout. And they'd just blank you. One time when I was quite young, at Leeds, I asked Dennis Bergkamp: 'Do you want to swap shirts after the game?'

'I don't swap shirts,' he said, just completely cold.

It made me feel even more inferior to him, which is to say he just fucking absolutely stomped me out like a cigarette. I thought, 'you bastard!' I hated him when I played against him after that. And I stopped asking people to swap shirts. I realised it might give them an edge over you.

Like Raul, Bergkamp used to play positions where you couldn't get near him. You couldn't touch him or do anything to disrupt his game; all you could do was try to read his passes and maybe intercept them. But it was hard. I remember Thierry Henry making a run and scoring from one of Bergkamp's passes. He was in that perfect number ten position and I couldn't go out to get tight. The pass slid by.

They were two great players on the same wavelength – well played – nothing you can do about it.

Shearer was another one you couldn't read. *What's he thinking? Have I got him now?* With 90 per cent or 95 per cent of strikers you can see if they've mentally thrown in the towel or not. But guys like him … you just never knew. Some wouldn't even acknowledge your existence. You try a little flick of the head; you try to make eye contact. Nothing. And not knowing is the worst thing. It's like when I was younger: if I got into fights it was always the quiet guys who worried me. Dealing with someone shouting and screaming? No problem. You know where he's at. He can come at me at 100 miles an hour and I'll be ready. But the guy who doesn't say a word, who doesn't even look at me, who shows no emotion … I have no idea what he's going to do. It's much harder.

Kevin Davies, Duncan Ferguson, Dion Dublin and Les Ferdinand. Sometimes I liked the direct battle. And sometimes I enjoyed *refusing* the battle. They'd try to run or jump into me or want me to elbow them … so I'd just play around them. I'd surprise them by letting them take a touch then hitting them with a tackle. When I was younger I was skinny and weighed ten stone wet, so there was no point going into a strength match with a Duncan Ferguson. So I might touch him on the left side of his back as the ball's coming into him. As he took a touch one way, I'd surprise him by coming the other side. I could do little tricks like that because I knew what I was up against. But the cold, clever, silent types? They were freaky.

Outside Interests

Where's my hoodie?

Over the last few years I've been exploring things I find interesting outside of football. Of course football remained my top priority. But life is short and there are lots of other things I've been discovering. Like a lot of footballers, my outlook used to be quite narrow. I had no real interests outside of football apart from clubbing. I was such a party animal that parts of my life between the ages of about 16 and 22 are a blur. That got me nowhere. Then I got a lot more professional. I became a dad and a husband as well. My horizons widened.

I never planned to get involved in the fashion business or in social media, or have a magazine and interview musicians and film stars. In each case, I just followed my instincts and was curious about how the world worked. For instance, I started a restaurant purely because one day a friend said: 'do you fancy starting a restaurant?' He said a place had become available in Spring Gardens. Was I interested? It was an Indian restaurant we both knew because we'd eaten there. It was a nice place, but it had an obvious flaw for the centre of

Manchester: it didn't sell alcohol! The owner wanted to get out of a lease so we looked into it and said OK, yeah, we'll take it over. We decided to turn it into an Italian and call it Rosso. That means 'red' of course, as in United, but the name doesn't hit you over the head with the fact. I didn't want to put my own name on it, or make it associated with the club. I wanted it to succeed on its own terms or not at all.

No one in my family had ever been involved the restaurant business before – but that was part of the attraction. It took a couple of years before it became successful and now it's doing well. The food is good, the place is always full and it's probably one of the most vibrant restaurants in Manchester. It even got voted Restaurant of the Year in the North West. When I was in Manchester I might go there twice a week or once in six weeks. But it's a great building with lots of character and I enjoy it there. The fact that it makes money is not the buzz. For me, seeing people enjoying themselves, and being able to sit with them and enjoy the food and the atmosphere in your own restaurant, is special.

Of course, I had a bit of a battle with the manager about it. As soon as Sir Alex got wind of it he called me in and said, 'What are you *doing*? I don't want you to have a restaurant. You'll be sitting at a bar with alcohol and all that stuff. You're a *footballer* ....!' To his ears it didn't sound respectable. Maybe he thought I would turn into an alcoholic. I suppose everyone at the club remembers George Best and his boutique on Bridge Street, and other players who had pubs or nightclubs. I tried to put the manager's mind at rest. I said, 'I'm not going to be making pizzas or serving drinks! It's just some of my

Above: With Michael Owen in the England squad for the World Cup in France, 1998.
Below: World Cup 2006 with Lampard and Crouch.

All photographs © Getty Images

Above: Me and Nemanja Vidić.

Below: Projects outside football: me and the press chatting at the Monaco Grand Prix in 2003.

All photographs © Getty Images

Above left: Playing at the World Cup in Japan, 2002.

Above right: In the prime of my career as captain at the 2010 World Cup.

Below: Sometimes you have to take your hat off to teams and show them the respect they deserve: that Barcelona team was simply the best I'd ever played against.

All photographs © Getty Images

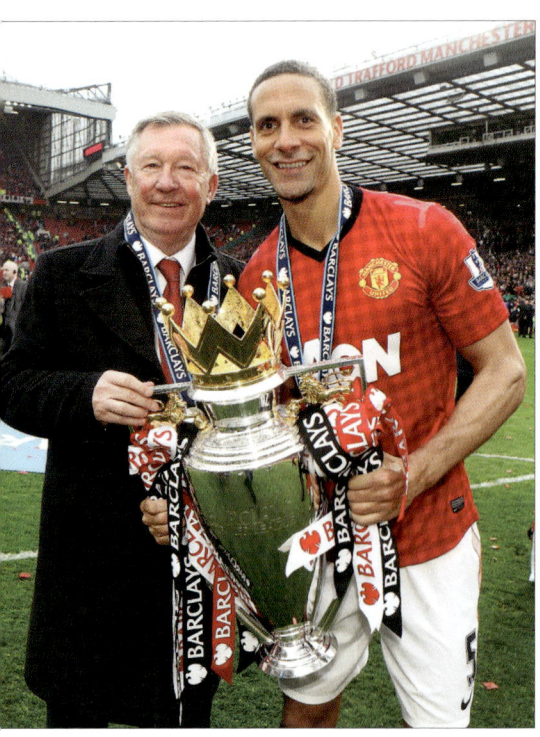

Above: Injured in 2010, it was a massive blow but time to reflect.

Below: A tale of two managers, one of which was eminently more suitable to the United way: when Sir Alex Ferguson retired (*bottom left*) we were confident we could continue his winning legacy at United, but Moyes' changes both on and off the pitch proved to be too much too soon (*bottom right*). All photographs © Getty Images

Above left: Me and Rebecca.

Above right: Me and my princess snuggling up on the sofa in front of the TV.

Below: My three children supporting me as I walk out for my testimonial match at Old Trafford. © *Getty Images*

Top left: My Mum and Peter, Sian and Jeremiah.

Top right: My Dad and Anton. © Getty Images

Middle left: Dad, Lisa, Chloe, Anya and Remy on their travels!

Below: Me, Jonny Evans, Michael Carrick and Nemanja Vidić arriving at Chester Racecourse. © Getty Images

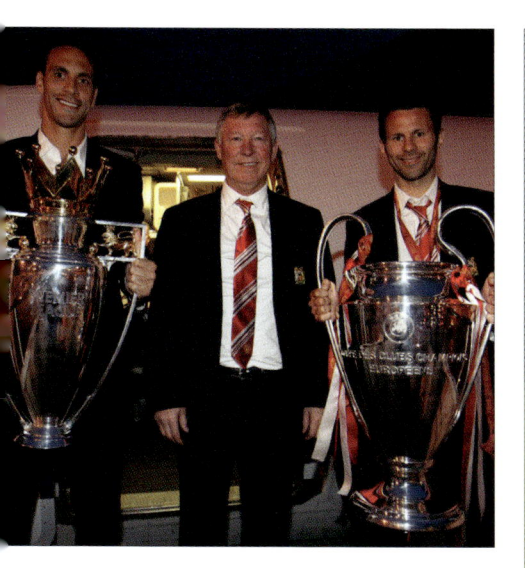

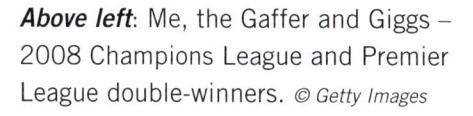

Above left: Me, the Gaffer and Giggs – 2008 Champions League and Premier League double-winners. © Getty Images

Above right: In training with Ronaldo. © Getty Images

Below left: 2014 in Rio with Dutch internationals Robin Van Persie and Nigel de Jong.

Below right: Playing for Leeds United. © Getty Images

Above: Me with the legend Diego Maradona.

Below: Me and Harry Redknapp at a QPR press conference in July 2014. © *Getty Images*

mates who are going to use my name and build it up. If it works, it works, if it doesn't it's just something that we tried.'

I'd thought it all through carefully. The most important thing was that it wasn't going to affect my football. In fact it would do the reverse. Instead of clubbing or going on betting sites or whatever, it would give me a nice interest. I'd reached the age where I knew exactly how to get myself into the best possible state of mind and physical condition to play. Football 100 per cent came first, and nothing ever interfered with that. Previously I'd always said 'no' to business propositions. But by my late 20s, I had worked out exactly what I needed to do to prepare for games. I knew what would be a distraction for me and what would be good for me. And at that point I said OK I can concentrate on outside things *as well*. I'm not sure I ever entirely won the gaffer round but once I had explained myself he never did anything to stop me.

In his book he talks about not approving of me doing stuff outside of football but he gets the story about P. Diddy slightly wrong. I'd done a programme with him before and he'd said he'd give me a shout when he next came to England. While we're in Denmark for a Champions League game P. Diddy calls me to say 'Hey, I'm in Copenhagen performing, can you come to the show?' I said 'no' because we had a game the next day so he said he'd come to the hotel, to meet the lads. It's a PR opportunity for himself obviously. He wanted a picture with the team. So I said alright and immediately went to the manager. I told him the idea and he's going *'Pee Daddy? What? Who?'* He'd never heard of him. Meanwhile, all the lads were going, 'Get him over, man! We want a picture!' I said, 'Boss, the lads want to see him and he wants to come over but he just wants to take just a picture and then he'll get off.' And he went 'Yeah, OK, no problem.' So that's what happened. He came, shook the gaffer's hand and everything, and that was that.

Ferguson saw the interviews and the magazine as a distraction. If I had a bad game or a couple of bad games he'd pull me in and say: 'What do you want to be? A fucking TV star or a singer … or a footballer?' And I kind of laughed it off because I knew it had no bearing on the way I was playing. I never let it interfere with training or preparations for a game in any way.

My #5 magazine and fashion stuff was much more of an experiment, more of a case study.

I started the magazine in 2010. Pete Smith at New Era suggested it. I said, 'Are you mad? Who's going to buy a magazine that I produce?' He said, 'No, no we'll do it online and we'll do it for free.' I said: 'how can you print a magazine for free?' And they explained the concept: it costs massively less online than printing hard copies. There is really no risk involved. And then you see how many people want to upload it. So I said, 'OK, all right. Let's try it.' I liked that it was free and environmentally friendly. So I thought, 'Let's have a go.'

At first the idea was just to try doing three editions over a six month period and see what happens. I would interview stars and those would be the main cover stories. The rest of the magazine would be written by other people. So the first one I did was 50 Cent, who at that time was the biggest rapper on the planet. I knew someone who knew him and he was in London, so I went and met him and we got on really well ... and the rest is history. Since then I have interviewed sports stars, musicians, people in film and fashion and I've loved every minute of it. I enjoy being out of my comfort zone. I'd never interviewed anyone before but here I was meeting people I respected from different fields. The interviews were filmed and I just asked what interested me: how did you get where you are? What stimulates you now? How do you prepare for a concert? What is your process? How do you come down after doing a concert with a hundred thousand people screaming at you? I have enough trouble getting back to normal after the high of playing a game of football: how do you cope?

I get to meet some of my heroes. These are people I'm genuinely thrilled to meet. Of course I get nervous because I'm a fan as well. My most nervous time was when I met Roger Federer the day after he'd broken the Wimbledon record for the most number of wins. I actually went in and sat with him and interviewed him for an hour! A whole hour! He loves football, he's seen me playing and he made me feel at ease. There was good banter between us. He's so graceful in everything he does. I love the way he carries himself, and there's a brilliant coldness about the way he plays and wins. The way he's sustained that over a long period makes me respect him even more. He's beautiful to watch, and I love that his one-handed backhand is a throwback to an earlier era. I think he saw my feelings of awe – I couldn't hide it – but he was warm and calm and gracious. And then he goes: 'If you ever want to come back or if you ever want some ...

some … um … my tennis shoes or anything like that just let me know.' And I'm thinking, 'Shit! This is *Roger Federer*!'

When I met Will Smith I saw the difference between a star and a *superstar*. You get 10 minutes with that guy and not a second longer! But he's warm, and he's *really* with you for that 10 minutes. Sometimes we're scheduled to do a 20-minute interview with someone and I get an hour. I could have sat with Jamie Foxx a whole day. Mickey Rourke's had an unbelievable life, so to read his story then be able to sit down and speak with him was unbelievable. When I met Usain Bolt after he broke one of his records I asked him what he eats and he goes: 'Chicken Nuggets. And I love dumplings.' I was like '*What?! Really?*' It was just like the people who ask me how I get around London and when I say 'By tube' they go '*What?! Really?*'

Meanwhile, we'd called the magazine '#5' because that's my number, and then that became a brand in its own right. It was an idea I had jointly with New Era. We thought: can this become a brand? The thinking went: we've got a logo, now what happens if we put it on something … like a cap? Why caps? They're simple. No one needs to try one on because one size fits all. And this was the experimental bit: 'let's do it purely on social media with no advertising or PR at all.' This was just about the time everyone was getting into Twitter, early 2011 or so. I happened to see a game on TV when Ray Wilkins was commentating and he kept saying 'stay on your feet … you gotta stay on your feet … he has to stay on his feet there.' He must have said that about 25 times! So I made that a hashtag of it. Whenever I saw someone lying down in an airport I'd take a picture, tweet it and put the hashtag on it: #stayonyourfeet. Someone did a slide tackle: #stayonyourfeet. I did it everywhere, and it became a meme.

When we went on tour to Asia I had my first foray into fashion: I had a load of 'Stay On Your Feet' T-shirts made. Amazingly, they sold out almost immediately, just through social media. Everywhere we went people were wearing the shirt and shouting in the stadium: 'stay on your feet, Rio!' I thought 'This is mad! It caught on so quick!' We'd sold so many T-shirts out of nothing so we thought: let's see if we can do something else through the magazine. We already had 500,000 subscribers and I had 2 million followers on Twitter, and about the same number on Facebook, so … we thought: 'Let's go!'

So I started promoting the caps. When I did an interview I'd give the person a cap. Some put them on. Some didn't. I wouldn't ask them to do it but I could say 'Here's a present … ' Jamie Foxx sat the whole interview with it on. Lewis Hamilton too. Nicole Scherzinger went and bought one! It had just been an experiment, but all of a sudden it was taking off. Every time we bring out a new colour cap it sold out. Next, we tried hoodies – and they sold out too. One time I went to Dubai and Tinie Tempah says to me, 'Rio, man, where's my hoodie?' While I was filming a World Cup preview with Olly Murs for the BBC he goes: 'Rio, I'm going on holiday with four mates and we all need caps!'

It's all gone so well that now I'm restructuring the business to do it properly to take things to another level. I've got all the big high street shops interested. Buyers from department stores are saying, 'Rio we want your track suits and your T-shirts!' But we have to take it carefully and make sure the clothes are good enough before we take that step.

We're just trying small runs of stuff at the moment to see if there's an uptake. Of course, there's a team around me at New Era who manage things day to day. But in terms of ideas, colours and styles I have to be involved.

Is this a new career? Probably not. With the fashion and the magazine and all the rest I'm still just exploring and playing. People give me ideas all the time. 'Do this,' or 'Dude, put money into that,' but at the end of the day it's my name and my reputation at stake. So far it's going well and hopefully it will continue to grow. But if it doesn't, we'll move on to something else. The main thing for me is that it's a good experience, learning about business, media, PR and so many other things. I never had time to go to college – but I'm learning my way.

Paul Scholes

The human sat nav

If Paul Scholes had the showmanship or outgoing personality of a Thierry Henry or a David Beckham there wouldn't have been a bigger star on the planet. Ask any of the greats in the game. Go to Barcelona and speak to the Xavis and Iniestas. Speak to Patrick Vieira. Speak to Zidane. Or go online and see what all those guys thought. They all say their hardest, most respected opponent in the Premier League was Paul Scholes. He is in everyone's top three. He was absolutely amazing.

He was always undervalued when it came to things like voting for Player of the Year because he was quiet. But here's something that tells you how highly thought of he was at Manchester United. He wasn't the best tackler and in training he used to kick people. But somehow no one ever said anything to him. If anyone else did the kind of things Scholesy did, they'd have been lamped! But everyone liked him and respected him so much he just seemed to get away with it. No one even seemed to mind too much when he got sent off. In one important game away at Inter Milan he got a red card after about ten minutes and you thought, well … that's not so bad because Scholesy's got us out of trouble loads of times. It was the same with the manager. He'd give Scholesy a long leash in a way he never did with other people.

That was because Paul Scholes was quite simply the best player who played for Man United. It was just a dream to play alongside him. He was just a great, *great* player. Everything he did was without fuss. But what he did was unique.

People talk about one of his trademarks: the long switch pass from one side of the pitch to the other. Yeah, there's a lot of players who can do a version of that. Lots of people can hit the ball from right to left or left to right. But there's very few who can do that and *take two or three defenders out of the game* at the same time! Scholesy did that continually. He never played the safe ball on the defender's safe side. He always played the ball to *hurt* the defender, taking him out of the game and putting our winger through on goal or into a position to cross unopposed. People talk about Xabi Alonso or Pirlo or Toni Kroos. Yeah, they're all great passers and everything, and they can play that ball as well. But they play it on the safer side. They don't play it as often or with such pinpoint accuracy as Scholes. He's The Human Sat Nav! Scholesy could score 30-yard goals in training that were just ridiculous beyond belief. Just have a look at some of them on YouTube. They're works of art.

He was always available. Always wanted the ball. No matter what the score was he wasn't afraid to come and get it. For me as a central defender he always gave me an option to pass the ball to, even if he was under pressure. You just can't put a price on someone like that. And at the same time he scored so many important goals. He did everything with such great integrity and quietness.

He is the most naturally talented player I've seen. You saw that in pre-season when we'd all been away for one month, six weeks or whatever it was. For everyone else it would be normal to take a couple of weeks to get their rhythm going again, to find their range in passing and shooting. Not Scholesy. He comes and on the first day he is the best player in training. Always. And he hadn't kicked a ball all summer! He still might be off the pace a bit but his technique and touch was like the day he left for his holidays.

After he retired, he came back and trained with us for a couple of days. We had no idea he was coming back until we saw him on the bus before a game against City. I said 'What you doing here?' He said 'I'm just coming to watch.' I said 'Oh, cool.' In the changing room the manager names the team ... and Scholesy's a sub. Fantastic! Scholesy is back! He hasn't played for seven or eight months but as soon as he starts training with us again he's the best player in training again! It was ridiculous. He went straight back into it at his old level.

I remember often running the length of the pitch to celebrate with him after a goal and saying to him 'This is just a pleasure, man! It's an honour just to play on the same pitch as you.' I used to say that to Giggsy as well. And it was. They would both do impossible things and just laugh about it! If that had been me or anyone else, we'd have been screaming and celebrating but he would just trot off like it was completely normal.

People didn't understand Scholesy. They thought he was bland but he could be one of the most cutting people I've met in football. He is not a vindictive person but every now and then he would make little comments or observations about people. Very dry. Very quick-witted. I never thought I'd see him on television, but when he appeared on Sky for the first time near the end of the 2014 season I thought: 'woah, he could open up on a few people here.' And he did. He laid into Arsenal, criticised Jack Wilshere, but was also critical of us. We were watching it together and the lads were laughing. What else could we do? It wasn't anything we didn't expect. Scholesy's an honest lad and he said what he thought. We couldn't complain because he wasn't wrong. We had to take it on the chin. He was just being honest.

Frankly

Thoughts on a friendship

I owe the Lampards a lot. Frank Lampard Senior, who'd been a great full back for West Ham in the 1970s and 1980s, scouted me for the club. Later the whole family welcomed me and helped me more than I can say. Frank Senior saw me playing for Blackheath District when I was 15 and he asked me to come to West Ham for a training session. I arrived about 45 minutes late because of the traffic and I hated it; I really didn't fancy going back. But he persisted. He came to see me again and told me the club was planning to invest money and time to find and develop young players and bring them into the first team. And he was true to his word: they made it happen for me. He used to pick me up from my estate – but would always have the doors of his black Mercedes locked when I came to the car. It made me laugh! What I never realised at the time was that Frank Lampard's son Frank Lampard Junior would become my close friend, teammate … and rival.

Frank Junior – I'll just call him 'Frank' from now to avoid confusion – was different from me in that he went to a private school, was very good academically and lived in a huge, luxurious house in Essex. But those sorts of things never came between us – we immediately hit it off. We were alike in our approach to football: both hugely competitive and deadly serious about improving as players. We were always the last two to come in after training. Harry Redknapp or the youth team coach Tony Carr would shout at us: 'Come in! Save your energy for the game!' and we'd hide and carry on playing where he couldn't see us. It wasn't exactly that Frank and I were trying out-do each other but there was a healthy rivalry and it was a part of our friendship. If he did some sprinting I'd think I can't *not* do that – I can't have him getting one up on me there! If he stayed outside for half an hour longer practising his passing or shooting, I'd think I should go and do some as well because I don't want him to get better than me at that. Frank's one of the hardest working professionals I've ever met – always doing extras, always working on his shooting and that's why, later, he scored so many goals.

We were good mates, but more importantly Frank was my driving force, my best *workforce* mate. We were both determined to reach the first team and always pushed each other in that direction, and, of course, we ended up playing for England together. But first we were apprentices and we played in the youth and reserves team together, before we broke into the West Ham first team. When he scored his first goal away at Barnsley we did a dance together to celebrate. We talked about it the night before: 'If you score, Frank, we've got to do a little dance.' It ended up as a really stupid jig. You look back at it now and think: 'What were we doing?'

FRANKLY

It wasn't all work. We roomed together when we travelled away and Frank was funny! He used to get up in the middle of the night – religiously – and have the longest wee I've ever heard in my life! I'm sure it was just to make me laugh. We were always going out to clubs and pubs together. We were so much a double act that if anybody saw one of us without the other they'd go: 'Where's Frank?' or 'Where's Rio?' There was a good group of us in the youth team. Frank was the poster boy and probably the girls' favourite at that time – but I had the banter, so we made a good partnership. Much later he became a real West End Chelsea boy. But at that time he preferred to stay in Essex.

He and his family really looked after me. Because it was such a long way from Peckham I used to often stay at their house, which was near Romford. When I first went I thought flipping hell! These people are living in sheer luxury. They were so warm and welcoming and generous. Frank's Mum Pat was an absolutely lovely lady – she was Lamps's diamond, really, and was brilliant with him. While Frank Senior provided the drive and intensity, she had this lovely soft touch: the encouraging mum you'd love to have. Frank really loved his Mum and looked up to her more than anyone. She made me feel so welcome and always looked after me, cooking unbelievable breakfast fry-ups for us on Sundays. And, well, everyone knows what happened with her: she suddenly fell ill and passed away. It was an absolute tragedy.

Meanwhile, Frank's Dad was pushing him and always being very strict with him, football-wise. When we played, you'd hear him berating Frank from the sidelines. If Frank had a bad game his father would provoke him: 'What's the matter with you? You didn't want the ball!' Yet one of the great things about Frank is he never goes into his shell. At the beginning, I think, his career was all about proving to his Dad that he could make it; being Frank's son was tough, after all. When he was young, Bobby Moore, his Dad's old teammate, used to pop round to their house for tea. And not only was Frank's Dad a club legend, his Uncle Harry was the manager (Frank's Mum's sister married Harry Redknapp). Frank could never escape being from football aristocracy.

Fortunately, Harry rated both of us. Whenever they needed a couple of youth players team to train with the first team he'd invariably call for me and Frank. Some of the older players used to give Frank a bit of stick for it – and, later, a lot of the fans reckoned he was getting preferential treatment because of his family. For instance the club arranged 'fan forums' at a conference centre: they were question and answer sessions with the manager, players and club officials. At one of these events a guy was hammering Frank, saying: 'He's not good enough! You're biased towards him because of who he is. There are better players in the reserves.' It turned out that the man's nephew was in the reserve team with Frank, but Harry came to his defence, saying: 'mark my words, this boy Frank Lampard will play for England, don't you worry about that!'

And of course he did.

Frank has had a great career and ended up outstripping the football achievements of his Dad. I was always a fan. Frank saw the game clearly and knew when and where to run and pass. He did everything quickly – one touch a lot of the time. But the word that defines him as a player is 'efficient': he was never interested in dribbling; pass and move was his game and he had this amazing ability at the edge of the box to shuffle his feet and get a shot off. He would make himself a bit of space and ... BANG! That was the product of years and years of hard work.

People argue about whether he or Steven Gerrard was the greater player. Stevie always seemed a bit more natural to me, but in terms of timing, getting in the box and scoring vital goals, there was no comparison with Frank. I always say if I were a manager, I'd take Frank every time: yes Gerrard can win a game on his own, and in his prime he won quite few like that. He won the FA Cup practically single-handed, and the European Cup Final against Milan in 2005. If I was paying to watch, I'd probably pick Gerrard because he's a bit more explosive and does a greater range of different things in a game. I'd watch him do things in training and in matches and think, fuck me, that's high-level! He'd hit precise, raking 30- or 40-yard passes like Scholes or Beckham. Or he'd drop a shoulder, beat someone and bang it in the top corner. He was explosive – he could get you out of your seat. Paul Scholes in his heyday is perhaps the only person who gets close to Frank in terms of timing his runs into the box from midfield. But, as I say, if I was a manager, I'd take Frank all day long. He was the coldest finisher in front of goal; he'd guarantee you 20 goals a season and you can't put a price on that. He'd get two chances in the game, score with one and the other one would be on target. Ridiculous! He broke the Chelsea goal-scoring record ... as a *midfielder*. That says it all.

Frank was so clever. He worked out that he'd get into the opponent's penalty area three or four times in a half, and the ball would fall to him once or twice, and he would score from one of those chances. He never had any weird or elaborate ideas about the game. He just played the odds: 'If I keep making these runs, I'll get one chance … and I'll score.' And he worked hard enough in training to make sure he was efficient and accurate enough to make that work. For five seasons for Chelsea he was scoring *20 goals a season. From midfield!* That's unbelievable. It can't be matched. He more or less won Chelsea the league one year, scoring two goals against Bolton on one of the last days of the season.

But the way our friendship went was difficult. And a lot of it was my fault.

When I left West Ham to go to Leeds we were still close but I was up the motorway so it wasn't easy to see each other. Things changed after he went to Chelsea in 2001, just as they were becoming a strong team; they were nowhere near winning the league back then, but their time was coming. I then went to Manchester United in 2002 and we became direct rivals. United won the league in my first year, then José Mourinho arrived and Chelsea won it a couple of times. We were now playing against each other.

Frank and I never spoke about it directly when we met up to play for England. But we were kind of drifting apart because of the United–Chelsea thing. If you'd asked me at the time I would just have put it down to a healthy rivalry of playing for the top two teams in the country. I wouldn't want to give him any information about what we were doing or planning because I'd worry he might feed that back to his team. And if Chelsea were winning I wouldn't want to speak to him anyway because I'd be jealous. I'm sure he felt the same way: he was competitive like me, and he always played his cards close to his chest. When we were winning, there'd been a little bit of 'I want that to be me, I don't want anyone else to win it.' I think it's just the way we're built.

It might have been even worse if he'd been at Arsenal because there was more animosity between us and them. But these days I see Patrick Vieira and Thierry Henry, and Martin Keown and we have a good laugh about old times. Hopefully that will happen with me and Frank.

It could just have been me. I know other people manage to maintain friendships with rivals. Wayne Rooney, for example, is good mates with Joe Hart. But I don't seem to be able to open up and be real pally with people I'm playing in direct competition with. I don't know why but I just can't do it. I felt the tension especially when we were with England together. If Chelsea had won the league, or beaten us in the cup or something I'd find myself sitting with Frank or John Terry or Ashley Cole and somewhere at the back of my mind would be the thought: are they fucking laughing at me? It's something they probably never felt at all. I only recognise it now as I'm looking back. Perhaps it's the dark side of being obsessed with winning. After all, you have to be a bit nutty to have that drive to keep winning trophies all the time. You don't want to show any kind of weakness. I wasn't even really aware of the feelings at the time. And they probably weren't laughing at me at all. But that was part of why it meant so much to me to beat them in the Champions League Final. I couldn't bear the thought of life afterwards if they beat us. I don't know if they ever thought like that or even imagined I was thinking those type of things. But, looking back I think: fuck me! That's how I was thinking! I don't think it was healthy and it strikes me now as a bit weird. Perhaps Frank felt something like that as well. But I do regret in terms of our friendship.

In fact I rather regret that I tended not to allow myself to have friendships with people I was in direct competition with. If anything other players were more like acquaintances. There were a couple of exceptions to that: I went on holiday a few times with Ashley Cole, but he had a very different personality: a happy-go-lucky kind of free spirit. But among the footballers who played in my era Jody Morris is my best mate in football and there are others I get on really well with like Michael Carrick. I'll definitely stay in contact with a lot of the United lads. Ian Dowie, who's a bit older than me, was a mentor to me at West Ham and we're still in touch. He's a nice fella; he looked after me when I was a young player, helped toughen me up. He's always been there for me if I needed advice.

At United I was close to Nemanja Vidić. We used to have a lot of deep conversations about football and life. But with a teammate it's different. You're not fighting against each other to win trophies.

Of course, outside of football I still have the same close friends like Gavin, Ray, my cousin Bernard and my agent Jamie. But they weren't competitors so there was no problem.

I can see now how I shut out most people or didn't really get involved after I went to Manchester United. I don't know how Frank feels because we never spoke about this and in fact I've only thought about it since I left United. He might feel completely differently. In his book he had nothing but nice things to say about me. He said we'd 'Lost a bit of that closeness we used to have' when I moved north but things were fine when we met up with England. Anyway, I hope now that we're not rivals any more things will change. We are both in our 30s now and even when I saw Frank at the England team hotel in Brazil I sensed a change. It was the first time we'd seen each other since we'd been released by our clubs and our guards had gone down. When we're back and both living in London I'm sure our friendship will develop again.

5.7 Million and Counting

The double-edged sword

It's the 2010 World Cup and I'm living the dream. All my injury worries are behind me. I'm feeling good, I'm feeling fit and I'm going into the biggest tournament on earth as captain of my country. It's our very first training session in Rustenburg and everything is going fine until the ball comes in and I go for it with Emile Heskey. It's an innocuous challenge and not Emile's fault, but as we go down, all his weight somehow falls on to my left knee. I remember shouting out at the time and Gary Lewin, the physio, runs over. I said: 'My knee, it doesn't feel right.'

In the ambulance on the way to the hospital, with the searing pain tearing through me, only one thing was going through my mind: that my World Cup might be over before it had even started. I asked the doctor if I'm going to be alright. 'I can't tell,' was his reply. 'If it's your ligaments, then you might not.' I began to cry. The first aid guy was looking at me in a funny way. As I get out on crutches, he says 'Can I have your shirt?' I just stare at him. How could anybody be stupid enough to ask me a question like that at a time like this?

I'm in pieces, waiting for my scan and trying not to cry anymore. Then all of a sudden the double doors open and a guy comes through completely smashed up, loads of blood everywhere. He's just had a car crash. That was the moment I accepted my situation. I just sat there and thought, 'You know what? I've got to start smiling, man, because compared to this guy I'm fine.' That gave me the sense of perspective I needed and I accepted the injury. It's not meant to be, so what can I do? A short while later the scan confirmed it. I'd strained my ligaments and it was going to take a month or two to heal. I thought, 'Well, that's it. I'd better move on.' And that *was* it. My World Cup was over but another world was about to open up for me.

I needed to get away so we rented a villa in Marrakech. I took my family, my agent Jamie and some of my other mates including Jody Morris. There was this new internet thing called Twitter which had started about eight months before in America and a few celebrities and sports stars there were into it. I thought, yeah, OK, maybe I'll just have a little dip into this … and … flipping hell! It was a revelation! I loved it! At first I thought it might just be a nice way to feel involved in the World Cup. But when I got back home it became a big thing for me in its own right. It enabled me to connect directly with fans. I'd had a pretty frustrating relationship with the media for years because the tabloids insisted on portraying me as someone I barely recognised. According to them, I was a party animal whose

5.7 MILLION AND COUNTING

only interests in life were red carpets, movie premieres and *bling*. I thought: why are they saying these things about me? They don't even know me.

Through Twitter I was able to show my real personality and real life. I started tweeting little snippets of my days. Even something simple like 'I'm doing the school run on the way to training' would get a reaction. *Really? Haven't you got a chauffeur to take the kids to school?* Er, no.

'I'm going to London on the train.' *You mean you don't have your own private jet or go by helicopter?* Er, no.

I'd tweet something from the train and people would go: '*Where are your bodyguards?*' Why would I need bodyguards? People have some pretty odd ideas about footballers' lives. Yeah, I really do wake up in the morning and go to work. I fix the kids' supper with our missus. I do the ironing every now and again.

Twitter also helped change the attitude of some of the United fans. I'd had quite a frosty relationship with some of them because a few years before I'd not signed a new contract immediately. It was normal for these negotiations to take a while: Roy Keane had taken a year; Becks more than a year. We'd only been talking for a couple of months when suddenly fans were telling me to sign the contract immediately. They reckoned the club had stuck by me when I had my ban. It was a fair point; but I had no intention of leaving United and negotiating details on any contract is normal, so why the fuss?

Unfortunately, in the middle of this, I was pictured at a table with Pini Zahavi, my agent at the time, and Peter

Kenyon, the Chelsea chief executive. I only bumped into him because I'd popped into the restaurant to see Pini for ten minutes. It was totally innocent. But someone took a picture and it went in the paper and it was made to look as if I was talking about going to Chelsea. The reaction of some of the fans was ridiculous! One night a big group of them came round my house wearing hoodies and baseball caps demanding to know why I hadn't signed a new contract. After a game at Charlton, as I walked off the pitch, they were bloody booing me! They were shouting 'Sign your contract! Boo! Go away! Until you sign your contract we don't want to talk to you.' My Dad was in the stand that day and almost got into a fight with a couple of fans over it.

I felt the fans hadn't even tried to understand what was going on and some of them carried on resenting me for a couple of years. They said I should be grateful to United. But people have to take the emotion out and understand that the game has become a business. Yes, it's a dream to play for Manchester United, but at the same time, United is commercially the biggest football club in the world, and the players have to be commercial too. Fans talk about loyalty and sentiment but it works both ways. If the clubs were loyal and sentimental to their players, then the players would be like that with the club. Yes, United supported me when I was 24, but how much of that was sentiment, and how much was it because I was seen as a valuable asset? They certainly weren't sentimental about dispensing with my services when I was 35. I don't think United fans would question my loyalty now. I was always a 100 per cent committed to the club. If I'd

5.7 MILLION AND COUNTING

had my way I'd have stayed until they had to carry me out. But that's not how the game works these days.

Being on Twitter has been amazing for me and has allowed me to connect directly with fans to avoid any misleading stories or rumors. At the time of writing I have about 5.7 million Twitter followers, and where United was once suspicious of this new medium, they've also embraced it in a big way themselves. I like to think I was a bit of a pioneer in the field! The manager used to worry that it might be a distraction from my football – but I was always totally clear it wasn't and never would be … and I think I proved that. I only ever did social media stuff in down time – in hotels before games, for example, or while travelling. In fact it was opposite – it's brought me a lot of joy and helped me with my football.

If we'd had social media when I was a kid, it would have been my dream to go on and be able to see what John Barnes got up to and to ask him how he trained and how he became such a good dribbler. Twitter allows fans to get that bit closer to the players. I know some players have their agent or their manager do their Twitter or social media accounts for them. But I think fans are cute enough to spot that. I write every one of my tweets myself and just try to give as much of a real account of what's going on as possible. I think that's why my relationship with fans has improved over the last four years. These days people judge me more from what they see on social media than what they read in the press.

The great thing about it is that it's a kind of giant never-ending conversation. It's not just me making pronouncements to the world – it's the interactions that are the most fun. I don't do direct messaging, but I've done loads of 'Q&As' and competitions where I'd let people win Xboxes or bigger prizes, such as a car or a box at an Usher concert. I love the interaction: every time I hit a landmark figure, like getting to 1 million or 2 million, I'd give away holidays. It was a way of giving something back to the fans. You have to remember Manchester United is a phenomenon all over the world and social media is a world wide platform too, so I'd be chatting to people from Africa, Indonesia – everywhere.

Plus there's loads of banter. It's like you get to actually chat with the fans who are shouting stuff from the stands during a match. But some of it gets quite mad. If you haven't got a thick skin, then, basically, don't go on Twitter. When you're playing well and your team is playing well, it's unbelievable and thoroughly enjoyable. You can take the mick out of people and it's sweetness and light. But – wow – if you're not doing well or the team hasn't done well, or you made a mistake … well, it's a hard place to be! It's a fickle world. There's loads of abuse and it can be a real confidence sapper. To be honest with you, when we lose, I've been known to give Twitter a miss for a couple of days!

Then again, fans are entitled to have their say. They care about their team, and they pay their good, hard-earned money to come to games and voice their opinions. That's part and parcel of the game these days. In the good times, they support you and they're unbelievable fans and in the bad times they can make you feel a lot worse than you should. But

5.7 MILLION AND COUNTING

that's fine. It's an emotional game and people should express those emotions.

I know exactly how fans feel because I'm an armchair fan myself when I watch rugby or boxing or even when I watch football. I can assure you the game is a lot easier from the stands. You're thinking: 'He should have been there … how has he not seen that pass?' I do it too, and it's part of the fun. But, trust me, it's a lot tougher down on the pitch.

Social media is a bit of a double-edged sword: you've got to be able to take abuse and accept it because if you retaliate or say something, you get fined. Actually, I think players should be allowed to come back and say a few things as long as you're not being vindictive or swearing or anything like that. It should be like in the changing room: if you dish it out you should be able to take it. If some geezer is absolutely hammering you for ages it would be nice to be able to shut him up a bit.

There are rules, however; the FA want players to be role models but the psychology is complicated. If some of the keyboard warriors who attack you all the time actually ran into you down the pub or walking in the street, they'd be the first to ask for an autograph or a picture. I think they insult you just to get a reaction. It's safer to have spats and banter with celebrities like Piers Morgan. He's an Arsenal fan and they weren't doing well for years so we used to cane him all the time. He's a bit of a fair weather fan too, so when it's going well, it's 'oh brilliant' and when it's going bad he wants Wenger 'out'. But it's all good knockabout stuff.

One thing that emerges is that some people don't seem to see us as human beings. They think of footballers as machines – and they make the excuse that they can do this because we earn lots of money. Football has always been a working-class game but because players are paid much more than 20 or 30 years ago, some people see us as no longer being working class. Some feel that gives them the right to abuse us. You get people who obviously think: 'You've escaped, but I haven't, so you're a fair target to vent my anger on.' I can tell you that the sort of people who dish out abuse would crumble if they were in our position. Their skin wouldn't be thick enough; they wouldn't have the personality to take some of the criticism about their family and friends. They couldn't take it, and they certainly wouldn't be able to bite their tongue and hold back as we have to most of the time.

What I can't stand are the crazy, vindictive people who just want to hurt and bully. For instance, I remember seeing a comment from someone saying: 'I hope you and the kids crash and die on the way to school,' or 'I hope you die of cancer.' One time I was going to Malaysia or Indonesia and someone sent the message, 'I hope the plane crashes.' Flipping hell, that's just mad, man! To be able to write that, you have got to be a real idiot or a there's something wrong with you. But that's the way things are: there are a few people like that out there, and when you find them they're usually some spotty little runt with no mates who's using social media to take out his frustrations on the world.

Wayne Rooney

Necessary devilment

Wayne Rooney took my breath away the very first time he trained with the England team. You could see immediately he was the real deal. He was physically ready, mentally cute, very aware of everything going on around him. After his first match against Turkey I remember going into the players' lounge and seeing him with his Mum and Dad. I said: 'So when are you coming to United then?' and they all laughed. But it was a serious question, and I'm so glad he did come.

In his first years with us he was like a coiled spring, always very animated and, it seemed, frustrated with life. He was rebellious, mischievous and funny. He struck me as a very angry young man, always arguing with people outside the training ground, especially on the phone. He seemed to fly into a rage about the smallest things and went through mobile phones like they were sweets. He'd just smash phones up in frustration. Just throw them on concrete. The other players used to laugh about it and say: 'He's gotta *calm down!*' I remember Carlos Queiroz walking past him in an airport when he punched his phone, threw it down and was generally going mad. Carlos couldn't believe it. He'd never seen anything like that. But in a way Wayne's anger worked for him on the field. I think it helped him become the player he could be.

Then he changed. In his early years he'd been petulant and reacted to everything on the pitch, and then, I don't know what happened, but he did calm down. Somehow he just clicked, and matured. Maybe it just came with getting older. Maybe it was something to do with having children. To be honest, I think he went a bit too far. He cared almost too much. He started saying things like 'I haven't been booked this season!' I remember thinking: 'Yeah, but you've not played as well as before either – you've lost something.' He was more aware of his image. The edge had gone and he was playing differently, thinking too much about not getting booked rather than going out and playing the game the way he could do it. I felt he needed that little bit of devilment in his game. I said to him: 'I'd rather see you get sent off once or twice and play the way I know you can play.' I think someone had spoken to him. Probably his agent or someone like that told him it would be better for him going forward. But football-wise I think he needed that old edge in his game. Not in his life obviously, but in his game. I think he lost that for maybe 18 months or two years maybe. That anger disappeared and his performances became less effective.

But after that he was top scorer, scored a hatful of goals up front on his own, as the number nine, which I think is his best position. And that season I thought: 'He's grown up now.' He started to work really hard, doing more shooting practice and stuff like that. I mean he did that before, but two or three years ago he started doing it with greater intensity and seriousness and with more method to it: workmanlike and honing his craft. He'd always done extras, but there's doing extras and doing extras. These days he tests himself all the time, does everything at match pace, not slow. He stopped taking a touch and having a look. Now it was getting the ball and ... Bang! Bang! I watched him and Juan Mata one day when they put on a clinic. They were unbelievable, hitting the net from all angles, never missing.

So in 2012 he was top scorer and then the following year he says, 'I want to play number ten. I prefer it. I'm better at number ten.' I said to him, 'You've just had your best year statistically and in terms of adulation and the media loving you. Why do you want to play ten??' He'd just elevated himself to a level just below the two best players in the world. He was just below Messi and Cristiano Ronaldo and I thought he could go on and improve and maybe join them. I'd put Inietsa, Xavi in that category, then there's probably a couple of tiers of players with players like Ibrahimovic, Suárez, Bale, Benzema, Pirlo, Robin van Persie.

By the way, all the talk of a problem between Wayne and Robin was nonsense. Sometimes statistics don't tell the real story. People noticed that one didn't pass much to the other in this game or that and decided there was a problem. I didn't see that. I saw two great players wanting to play well with each other.

But what I found strange was that year Wayne Rooney decided he wanted to play number ten and I just couldn't understand it! For me his best position is still number nine: when he's in and around the defenders' feet he's cute. He shoots back across defenders and through their legs like Ole Gunnar Solskjaer. He does tight little turns. He knows exactly where to be in the box. He's become a sniffer as well as a scorer of extraordinary goals. His little movements to make space for himself are so clever.

He does things other players can't even imagine. Little chips over keepers, unbelievable volleys from distance like the West Ham goal, or the Newcastle goal. I was in the stadium when he scored the overhead kick against Man City which was voted the best ever Premier League goal. I'll never forget that. I just stood up with my hands on my heads and said, 'What the hell just happened?' Don't get me wrong. He can still play a killer pass. He's still one of the top assist makers in the league. I just think he's more effective up top. I think under the management of Louis van Gaal we will see the return of the Wayne Rooney who terrorises opponents.

Mums and Dads

Thoughts on love

I was a bit of a difficult so-and-so for a couple of years after Mum and Dad split up. They'd grown apart but they never explained anything to me and I blamed Mum for it. I thought it was her decision. One day when I was brushing my teeth and washing my face in the bathroom my Dad came in and said: 'I'm going to be gone for a little while.' I replied 'All right' and didn't think anything of it. A few months then went past. 'Is he coming back or what?' I asked and Mum said 'No.' After that I made life difficult for her. I wouldn't listen, I was a bit disruptive and then she … One night I heard a man's voice. It was in the middle of the night about two or three years after Mum and Dad split up. We lived in a tiny flat so I could hear it clearly. I came out of my bedroom and walked into the living room to see a man sitting on the sofa and my Mum sitting on the other sofa. I went 'Who's this?' And she went: 'just go to bed. I'll speak to you in the morning,' and I said, 'No, just get this guy out of the house.'

From that day I was difficult. I told my Dad straightaway and he went mad. There were a few scenes. It was difficult for my Dad to see another guy in the house with his kids. Now I've got kids of my own I can understand why he was upset. I just never gave the new guy, Peter, a chance. I'd say to him, 'It's my remote control. Give me that. It's my TV. You're not part of this house' and stuff like that, which put Mum in such a bad position. She'd met someone after a few years of being alone and I was making it ultra difficult for her to have a relationship. One day at my auntie's she just broke down and said, 'Listen, you've got to understand!' That led to a long talk about relationships and how things just don't work out sometimes. And it was just … it was one of those good conversations and I felt bad. I thought 'I've been acting like an idiot.' From that day on, while I didn't automatically like the guy, I was going to respect my Mum's decision that she needed to have a life as well. It was a big moment really.

A couple of years later my Mum married Peter and I made a speech saying 'listen, as long as you look after my Mum and make her happy, then I'm happy.' And he has done. He's been perfect for Mum. He's been brilliant. My Mum couldn't have met anyone better. And we get along great with him now. He's bought into the family: he's a football fan now, he loves Man United and he's great with my kids. He's become a terrific grandparent. Meanwhile Dad met someone else too – Lisa – and I must admit I made it a lot easier for her to get into the family. At first I had reservations about her. 'She's not my Mum. What's she doing here?' But it was a quicker transition than for Peter. So the family is much bigger now.

MUMS AND DADS

There's me and Anton of course. Then there's Sian and Jeremiah, Mum's children with Peter, and Lisa's children with Dad who are Chloe, and the twins Anya and Remy. And I have to say Lisa's been great as well.

Ultimately, I think it's all broadened my understanding. I know why there were so many problems in the past, and I understand a lot more about how the dynamics of relationships affect kids. When my Mum and Dad were together I always used to say I was the lucky one in my class. Until they split up, and then I was thinking: my Mum and Dad are the same as everyone else's.

Dad could quite easily have gone and lived in another part of the country. In fact he thought about going back to the Caribbean. But I was lucky that he made the conscious, concerted effort to stay around. He moved to the next estate so although he was no longer in the house he was still ever-present in my life — so, emotionally I wasn't too badly affected. Perhaps if he had moved away I would have had a bigger reaction. Dad went out and worked all the hours God sent, all over London, and was always around for me. Sometimes you see kids who turn to drugs and drink and various vices and, when they look back, they blame it on the moment when one of their parents walked out and left them. So I'd say I was fortunate, in that he didn't give me that excuse.

I never believed in marriage until I had kids of my own because my Mum and Dad never got married. I thought that was the norm. But now I realise it's a good thing for everybody concerned. And that's why I got married, and because I love

Rebecca, of course! I never did counselling or therapy or anything like that. I just worked it out myself, really. But now I'm a Dad. I've got a lovely family and I'm totally committed to sticking with that and making that work. I'm sure that comes from my own experience as well. Mum looked after other people's kids and looked after us, and moved heaven and earth to make sure we got to places on time. We went to school. We went to youth clubs. My auntie ran a youth club in New Cross not far from where we lived and Mum made sure I got there. Mum cooked and cleaned, and made sure I didn't miss out on anything. She was just a massively good, hard-working, devoted mum.

No one really got married in my family so it was never really on my agenda. But then I had kids and what bigger commitment is there than that? I don't know what it was but it just seemed like a natural progression to get married. I think when you're in love with your kids and your family life and your girlfriend – as Rebecca was for me at the time – it is just a seamless transition.

I always feel like I'm still pretending to be an adult. It's like the old saying that you never grow up. You never feel that you're completely grown up is where I'm at. I think that keeps me young! You don't get a book that tells you how to be a parent. No one tells you how each kid should be fathered. It's all work in progress. But when I look at my three kids and I sit there and think, 'wow! How have I created these?' It still feels like it was only a couple of years ago that I was back at school. Time flies when you're having fun. I love being a human climbing frame for my kids to clamber all over me. I love

MUMS AND DADS

how, no matter what's happened at work, no matter what's happened in a game, you come home and the kids just look at you as their dad. There's nothing else. I love looking after them. The responsibility of having to take care of someone else is a nice thing to have. But Rebecca is the one who makes it all function. She is a great Mum. She's the one who makes sure everything is in the right place and at the right time. She's the one who makes sure the kids are up and doing what they are meant to be doing and eating and bathing and going to sleep. She's the one who makes it all work.

I still look at the young boys now and listen to their stories and think, yeah, I wouldn't mind once every few months going out and partying. But I had my time. I had a good time doing that but that was a different phase in my life and this is a different time now. It corresponds a bit to the change in my football life as well. The more professional I've got over the years coincided with having kids. I'm not stupid enough to think that everything's perfect now or that I'm perfect. I'm going to make mistakes and wrong decisions in future. I know that. But I try and learn.

One of the great things about Rebecca is that she's not one to talk about football. She doesn't care about it. If you've won she's happy, but she doesn't want to know the details and that suits me. It's easier for me because I can switch off when I come home. She's never been interested in fame or anything like that or the WAG lifestyle. She doesn't want to be in the papers or do photo shoots. And that's good, too. It avoids putting any more pressure on the kids. We've been together a long time now. We met when she was 18 and I was nearly

21. We've had our ups and downs like every relationship. But we've had a great time and grown up together. She's matured, I've matured and we've grown into being parents now. We look at each other sometimes and think, wow, we're actually great at this! I thought we were just still playing at this, that it's a game … but it's not.

Ronnie and Leo

Arrogant?
Rubbish!

Who is the best player in the world? New pretenders will stake their claims. But for the last few years only two names have been worth serious consideration. One of them is a friend of mine. The other is a genius I faced in the two most painful games of my career and I'll never forget how good he was.

Before I give my verdict on Cristiano Ronaldo and Lionel Messi, the most important thing to say is that they are both extraordinary professionals. They didn't get where they are without years of dedication. Some kids envy their trappings of success – money, cars, beautiful girlfriends and all that. But you have no chance of becoming a star if that's the stuff you're thinking about. Leo and Ronnie are fantastic examples of guys who are motivated by something else: passion for the game, the desire to improve, and the determination and hunger to work hard and improve to make it happen. I think both of them have incredible determination, but show it in different ways.

Ronaldo is the best example of a *self-made* great player. Don't get me wrong. He was born with fantastic natural talent. But it's his work ethic that took him to the top. He is one of the hardest workers I've ever seen. I remember watching him soon after he arrived in Manchester. After training he would pick up a bag of balls, and almost shyly walk over to the other pitch, as if he'd be embarrassed if people knew he was going to do extra work. Then he'd put little weights on his ankles and practise free kicks, step-overs and other skills. After a while you started seeing the results. He was getting more powerful, growing into his physique. He was a workaholic, but it didn't stop there. He lived a couple of doors up from me so I'd see him at his house. He had a special chef to cook the right type of foods. He invested in that himself. And he had a swimming pool so he could do special stretching exercises. Everything about his lifestyle was geared to becoming the best footballer in the world, which he wanted to be and which he achieved.

He learned. When Ronaldo first arrived Ruud van Nistelrooy was the main man at United. Everyone loved him because he scored so many goals. Then this little young, skinny Portuguese boy with funny hair comes along with his step-overs and dancing and the crowd loved him. One day in training Ronnie was taking the mick out of the left back, beating his man then going back and beating him again. Ruud was furious and started shouting: 'Cross the fucking ball! How can I make runs when I don't know when you're going to cross the ball?' Ronaldo was like, 'But I'm doing skills, what's wrong with you?' But Ruud said, 'I can't play with this guy,' and walked off. There were a couple of incidents like this before Ronaldo understood: he realised you're always going to be respected more for being effective than being a show pony. It takes intelligence to understand that the game is not all about skill. I used to tell him to concentrate on end product. I loved the stuff he did. But I liked it better when it produced a cross or a shot. He went on to become more than effective. He became lethal. He developed every aspect of his game. He had all the attributes. If he could put it together he was going to be devastating. And he's never stopped developing. He still keeps adding new things to his game because he's constantly thinking about it. He's always analysing: 'What is going to make me the best player in the world?' And he worked out what that was: assists, goals, being *decisive* … and turning up in the big games. That's why he breaks records and why he was voted World Player of the Year in 2014.

Some people think he's arrogant. Rubbish! Listen a bit more closely to the criticisms and you'll see what they're really about. Of course there's a debate to have about who's the best. But some people say Messi purely because Ronaldo is good looking. Their wives and girlfriends are probably thinking 'I'd love to go out with Ronaldo,' but they don't think that about Messi. So he's not a threat! Ronnie's got all the cars, all the money God can send. Good looking. Physique? Ridiculous! What more does he want? He can't be the best player in the world as well! So I can't say he's the best as well! Jealousy is what it boils down to sometimes.

Everybody who slags Ronaldo off is actually doing him a favour. He almost needs to have people saying Messi is better.

It drives him on. You see it in the defiant way he celebrates: 'I *told you*!' People mistake that for arrogance. It's more like: 'I told you! You better believe in what I'm doing.' It's not 'I'm better than everyone else!' He's just not like that as a person at all.

People didn't understand his celebration at the end of the 2014 Champions League Final when he scored the penalty to make it 4–1 for Real against Atlético, and then took his shirt off. People complained, 'Oh, he shouldn't have done that. He is taking attention away from the other players.' No, he's not! You don't know. That celebration was pure emotion. He would've been thinking, 'If this final finishes and I've not scored a goal, I will look at that as an embarrassment.' He wanted to make an impact on that game. That's what I saw in his reaction. It was: 'I've scored! Now I can celebrate properly!' That's the sign of a *great* player not an egotistical one. In my experience he's not self-centred or arrogant at all. At United he was always involved in the jokes. Whatever was going on in the changing room, he'd be involved. Quinny – Quinton Fortune – used to batter him about his hair, clothes. But he'd always fight back. 'Oh you English have no style.'

Between Messi and Ronaldo, Messi is the more naturally talented. He's a genius, a magician in a way that Cristiano isn't. You can tell the difference from the way they score goals: power or precision. Messi's goals are like fine art. He curls the ball in. He's measured, precise, delicate. He's all about guiding the ball into the corners. Ronaldo sometimes hits the ball and he wouldn't even be able to tell you where it was going, except that it would be somewhere on target. He's *forcing* that ball into the back of the net. They're both great to watch, just different.

If you wanted to build the prototype of the perfect footballer, Ronaldo would be it. He has physical power, incredible pace and uses both feet whereas Messi is mainly left footed. He scored a header against us in the Champions League but that is very rare for him. Ronaldo scores every type of goal: long-range, poaching, free kicks, penalties, headers like Duncan Ferguson or Bob Latchford. His flying header against Roma in Rome was just crazy. He jumps from the edge of the box, and heads it on the penalty spot. It took your breath away. And it was fearless too: he got hurt scoring that one. And his goal against Porto was even more amazing. I remember realising he was about to hit it and thinking: 'No, no, that's impossible' because he was 40 yards out. And it went into the top corner!

With Messi, you get the feeling that this guy was always destined to be one of the best in the world. He's obviously had to work hard but everyone knew about Messi before he even played in the first team. I remember Ronaldinho – who was the best in the world at the time – saying in an interview that this kid was going to be the best. That was unprecedented: the world's top player passing the baton like that. On Messi's debut, Ronaldinho was just trying to put the kid in on goal to score a goal every time he got the ball!

But Messi has had to fight too. He is small. He had a lot of injury problems at a young age. But he's so good technically he can get past you in many different ways. He can unbalance you with just a drop of the shoulder. His acceleration is phenomenal. And he's still taking the game to another level, statistics-wise and by dominating games and scoring ridiculous goals. They said 2014 was a bad year for him: he scored more than 40 goals and led Argentina to the World Cup final! He's more reserved whereas Ronaldo has the showmanship to be the main man, to be the guy that everyone sees and looks at, and who shows all of his emotions on the pitch.

Neither of the two dominated the World Cup in Brazil as they would have hoped. Messi got to the final but he didn't really set things alight. He won the award for best player of the tournament although he obviously wasn't the best player. Maybe it was something to do with the sponsors. He looked almost embarrassed when he had to go up and collect his award after the final. On the other hand, he definitely had a better World Cup than Ronnie who would have had targets he wanted to achieve, and he never got anywhere near them. I spoke to him after the tournament and I could sense he was gutted, though we didn't talk about it directly.

So who's the best? It's still hard to say. If I was the manager and was going to buy a player for Man United I'd go for Ronaldo because he's accustomed to the Premier League, and he scores all types of goals. He can score a goal that Duncan Ferguson can score. He can score a goal that John Barnes would score. He'd score a goal that Gazza would score. He does it all.

But then I'm biased because I played with Ronaldo for years. Thierry Henry, who played with Messi at Barcelona, had a different take on it. When interviewing him during the World Cup for my #5 magazine I asked him who was better. He said he respected and admired Ronaldo but then told me why he thinks Messi is the best ... There was an incident during a practice match when Messi got fouled and the coach, instead of giving a free kick, said to play on. Messi was livid, so when the ball went back to his goalkeeper, he ran back and demanded it. The goalkeeper rolled him the ball, and Messi then proceeded to run through the entire team and score in anger. Thierry said that was what he used to do in the playground at school. I did stuff like that too against little kids. But Messi did it against some of the best in the world: Yaya Toure, Puyol, Iniesta, Xavi, Busquets. And it wasn't just that one time. He did it a couple of times. Thierry said: 'Can Ronaldo do that?' I said, 'Well, I've never seen him do that.' Thierry played with Zidane and Ronaldinho but they never did anything like that. He said, 'That's when I knew Messi was different to anyone we've ever seen.' I have to admit I was too stunned even to say 'Wow.'

My Foundation

A sense of perspective

If I hadn't been a footballer I would probably have been a community youth worker. My Mum and Dad were always very giving people, always helping people on the estate and the estate was community-based, with loads of youth workers. So I thought: if I don't make it as a footballer that's what I'll do. I'll work for the local council with all the kids. That's what a lot of my friends do today, so I'm sure I probably would have fallen into that kind of work myself.

As kids, we'd sit on the stairs and everyone was always saying: 'you know what? If I ever make it, there's no way I am going to be a sellout and disappear. I'll come back here and help.' We all said that and it stuck with me. All my mates from that time help in the community one way or another. A lot of them moved away from Peckham, and have different jobs, but they've all kept strong ties to the area we grew up in.

When I was a young player at West Ham there was loads of community work to be done and I got involved with the Prince's Trust, visiting projects, giving out awards and stuff, encouraging kids to get qualifications and get their lives together. The Trust is something I really believe in. It gives kids an opportunity to start a new life if they put the effort in. A few years ago I was talking about this with an old mate and he said: 'why don't you start a foundation yourself. You could raise a lot of money and change a few people's lives.' And he was right. So that's what I've tried to do. It's developed over the years and is now called the Rio Ferdinand Foundation, and we've helped a few thousand children who've gone through our projects.

We take a similar approach to the Prince's Trust: giving kids the self-esteem, confidence and qualifications to start a new life. One aspect is to show them there are lots of different ways to make a living in fields they love. Lots of kids, for example, love sport and music and entertainment. They can't all be the next Rio Ferdinand, or Wayne Rooney, or Olly Murs, or One Direction. But there are loads of other jobs in and around those industries. So we try to show them the possibilities, encourage them to explore and fulfill their talent, and open their eyes to what they are capable of. The way the foundation works is to help kids get their qualifications, and make it possible for them to start climbing the ladder and hopefully they'll end up working in those fields. We have had a few kids working in film now. I produced a film called 'Dead Man Running,' and a few of the foundation kids worked as runners and now about six of them have jobs in the film industry.

From my point of view, being involved in work like this gives you a sense of perspective. As football players we can be

MY FOUNDATION

moaning about silly little things: 'Hey! Where's the shower gel! ... The pasta is overcooked!' Like everyone else, we get absorbed in our own little worlds a lot of the time. But when I go to one of our courses and hear some of the kids telling their stories, well, that really puts things in context. I remember one boy from Hull who was at rock bottom. He'd fallen into a great big hole and he didn't see any way out. He'd been kicked out of his family home, he was homeless, he was drinking and taking drugs and he was suicidal. One of the few positive things in his life was that he loved football. He joined a community programme coaching and mentoring young kids and the transformation in him is just amazing! He got his qualifications and now he's coaching football in the community and has become a mentor himself, helping younger kids get qualifications of their own and get on the ladder like he has. Now he's doing well by himself and he's just about to go to South Africa to do a coaching course. A few years ago this guy couldn't even imagine travelling to a different city in England. Now he's flying halfway across the world!

Even more harrowing, I remember a young girl from Salford talking about how she had to run away from home because she was abused sexually by her Mum's various boyfriends and had nowhere to live. Eventually, she was taken in by foster carers and came to the Foundation. She had a lot of stuff to work through but now all the other kids look up to her and she's an inspiration to others. She works for the Foundation as a mentor and goes around the country doing courses.

I hear those kind of stories and think 'flipping hell. The Foundation is doing some really good work. I didn't realise it was going to get this deep.' I'm very happy that it does but it reminds me of what I knew as a kid on the estate. A girl got stabbed to death once on the stairwells. Someone else got shot. I knew girls that got raped by older men on the estate. This is what I grew up around. It wasn't ever far from my front door. I know all this. But then I got detached from all that by being a footballer, and having tunnel vision, not letting anything get in the way of me becoming a professional player. You don't think about this stuff – then all of a sudden your memories come back and you think: that shit still goes on. And you have the urge to try and make something better for at least a few people.

I don't often talk about it, actually. People say 'oh, he's only doing it for himself, for PR, blah, blah, blah.' On the other hand, charities do need a certain amount of celebrity to focus attention on a problem and help raise money, so when you become a footballer you've got to use that leverage to actually get issues noticed and make people aware that there is still some shit going on that does need help. I'd love to talk about this stuff in every interview I do but I don't want people thinking it's about me rather than the charity, so I don't bring it up. You have to find a balance but that's difficult because we live in such a cynical world.

I was lucky to find a guy called Gary Stannett who's now our chief executive. He's been in this industry for years. The way it works is that he gives me an update probably every two to four weeks. He tells me what's going on and we discuss new ideas. Should we run a new course on such and such? Should we work with this or that organization? I'm always in touch

MY FOUNDATION

with what is going on and these days my Mum is involved quite a lot as well. She's organised fundraising auctions and gala dinners in the last couple of years.

It's a good feeling. Part of it is getting auction prizes and stuff to go to my friends in the entertainment world and getting the kind of things that money can't buy. I might ask Jimmy Nesbitt or someone to come in and do an appearance or presentation or a speech for the charity. And these guys are like me: just normal people who've done well in their industry but still have got their feet close to the ground.

We run courses and projects in Salford, South London, South Africa and Uganda. We are just starting a partnership now in Northern Ireland, in Belfast. Unfortunately, I can't get to all of them because football is my bread and butter, but when I do get the time and opportunity I do love to get more involved and have a look at what's going on on the ground.

It's all part of being proud of where I've come from and connecting with that. I never try to hide the fact of where I have come from. I like it. I enjoy it. I love it. Growing up in Peckham made me who I am today, so I love to go to familiar places to get some Caribbean food, say, or a haircut. Certain people say, 'What are you doing there man? You shouldn't be around here. It's dangerous.' They don't understand that I feel good in places like Lewisham in London, or Moss Side in Manchester, or Lozells in Birmingham. Why should I be scared? These places are mirror images of where I am from in London, so I always feel comfortable. There's a big Jamaican presence, and a real mixture of people: white, black, Somalians, Africans, lots of different cultures, which is exactly how I grew up.

There was a great place I used to go to get my hair done in Moss Side called Ritchie Barbers, which is still there. For five or six years I went to a dread guy called Raheem on Tipp Street. He's a good guy, too, a typical Manchester lad. And then I went to Chris Rock, a Jamaican guy who's also in Moss Side. One time in Lozells me and Emile Heskey walked into a place together and people were like 'whoa, what are you doing here?' So I said: 'I've come to get a haircut, man. What are you doing here?'

Life After Football

When you're young
And everything's going your way

It comes to us all in the end – but it still takes you by surprise. A couple of days after Ed Woodward had sat down next to me in the changing room at Southampton and surprised me by telling me United wouldn't be renewing my contract, I went shopping at Waitrose in Alderley Edge. As I walked to my car I heard chatter behind me. A Dad and son had spotted me and were having a conversation:

'Do you know who that is?'

'Yeah, that's Rio Ferdinand.'

'That's right. He used to play for Manchester United.'

Used to play? It was like hearing my own obituary. It hadn't actually hit me until that moment that my Manchester United career was dead. But I was determined to carry on somewhere else. I love football too much to call time on being a player. Manchester United no longer wanted me but I had offers from clubs all over the world.

I opted to connect again with my first manager Harry Redknapp and signed to play under him at QPR, where I'd trained as a teenager before joining West Ham. I told Harry: 'I started with you and I'd like to finish with you.' The key word of course – there's no dodging it – is 'finish'. Every athlete has that moment of truth where age catches up with him or her and they have to stop doing the thing they love. I'm not quite there yet, but I know the moment is not far off.

The problem is that footballers, like other athletes, are not usually prepared or educated to deal with normal life after they retire. That's why you see the stories of great athletes like Mike Tyson and so many others who've worked their whole careers and when they retire, fall into financial trouble and depression. Retirement is an important subject but it's hardly ever talked about. It is almost taboo. But I'd like to talk about it because it can hit players hard and I wish there were more opportunities for players to think about life after football and how they can prepare for what is a massive change.

Many footballers have a kind of 'Peter Pan' lifestyle and the end of their career comes as a shock. They think they are useless to society; they don't know anything outside football and they don't have the life skills to cope with new problems. But while their life as a professional footballer may be over, they've still got their whole life ahead of them. You usually finish football in your mid- or late 30s. But you'll actually live to you're mid- or late 80s – that's another 50 years. So players need to think ahead, make investments and new careers for themselves.

I'm lucky; I am well prepared. I've had help and been able to think about and work towards this moment for

LIFE AFTER FOOTBALL

years. I've got my charitable foundation, my media work, my restaurant and other businesses, my social media … if I hadn't had all these things going on in my life when I had my injury problems and was upset over losing the captaincy of England and United, God knows what would've happened to me. Maybe I would have turned to drink or gambling or depression might have set in or who knows what else. But that didn't happen and for that I have to thank a number of people, most especially my friend and agent Jamie Moralee.

Jamie and me go back a long way. He's a great fella who's been through hard times but has managed to turn negatives into positives for himself and others. We first met in the late 1990s when I was a teenage defender on loan at Bournemouth and he was a striker in his mid-20s with Crewe Alexandra. We played against each other a few times after that and we ran into each other on holidays. It was always a pleasure to run into Jamie: he and I would go to clubs and pubs and have long conversations as well. Then our paths diverged for a number of years and I didn't see him again until our mutual friend Jody Morris' wedding about eight years ago. By then, I was in my prime at Manchester United and Jamie had become an agent. Meeting up with him again was one of the turning points in my life; it's worked out to be a blessing for both of us.

My financial and managerial situation off the pitch at that time had become a mess, and I'd given no thought at all to the future. My football agent was Pini Zahavi, who I'd been with years and had been fantastic for me since I was a young player. Another agency handled my commercial deals, someone else booked my holidays, another guy looked after my finances, and there were other people for insurance and my property. It didn't really make a lot of sense.

Meanwhile, since we'd last met, Jamie had gone through bad times but had become a person who used his bad experiences in football to help others. At the age of 21 he'd been considered one of the best strikers in England outside the top division. He'd had a half-million pound transfer to Watford but hadn't known how to handle the pressure. He lived too fast and succumbed to the temptations of overspending and over-indulgence in nightclubs and his playing career nosedived. I've always been lucky to have people outside football to turn to for wisdom, such as my best friend Gavin or my wife or my parents or Anton. But Jamie never had anyone to give essential advice on football and life. He wasn't the only one to suffer from lack of guidance: a lot of my contemporaries were talented footballers who'd not had quite the career they should've done for one reason or another.

By the time we met again, Jamie had built an agency that aimed to help players by taking a wider and more long-term view of a player's life and career. As we renewed our friendship, Jamie talked about player management and explained the principles of things like helping players to make intelligent investments. I saw how he was around the England boys at our hotel: all the lads liked and trusted him but what drew me to him was the clear vision he saw for me in terms of building me as a 'brand' and, more importantly, for helping me prepare for life after football.

Jamie persuaded me to join him in his company where

LIFE AFTER FOOTBALL

all my interests and needs would be under one roof. He'd look after all that but at the same time he'd make me more business-minded and help me educate myself so I would never again leave my financial affairs in the hands of other people. A lot of footballers simply take advice from their financial advisers and sign on the dotted line when someone says 'Don't worry, it's a great investment.' I've made a couple of bad calls on deals here and there, but that's life. I am now involved from start to finish in everything I do because that's the way I wanted. And I'm grateful to Jamie for helping me to get to that point. He's someone I liked and trusted. We've never looked back and I'm now an ambassador for his company, New Era.

Jamie has a unique take on some of the problems that footballers face. I'll let him explain in his own words:

Football is such an unusual sport. There's no other industry in the world where your earnings can fluctuate so wildly. Someone in a normal job might be earning £20,000 a year, then get an upturn and earn £26,000. That's manageable. But as a footballer you can be playing in the Premier League earning £60,000 a week and you can't see past the diamonds and the cars and the adulation. Suddenly, you get an injury, and even though you are still doing exactly the same job you can find yourself on £5,000 a week. But the lifestyle stays the same and you've suddenly got mortgages for more than you're earning. How do you adapt? Your skills haven't changed; you are still in the same industry and you can still be playing in front of tens of thousands of fans. So how do you mange that downturn in wages? Then at the age of 35 you have to retire and you're unemployed. Nothing in your experience prepares you for that.

It's no wonder so many footballers have gone bankrupt. There'll be many more in future, too. Players think they will stay young and that football is going to be there forever. On the 28th of every month money goes in, and then comes the day when no money goes in. Suddenly all those people who've wanted to be your friend, who've been begging you for tickets for the last ten years, don't even pick the phone up. They've moved onto some new star. Down the pub it goes from 'What are you having?' to having to buy your own drink. Around the age of 37 can be the most difficult. You look at yourself in the mirror and think: 'Fuck! What has happened to me? Five years ago I was on TV and in the papers every week and being loved by 40,000 people in the stadium and now no one even knows who I am.'

Worst of all, you have no support network. I've known players who earned £30,000 to £40,000 a week for ten years and at the age of 40 they're struggling to put a pair of trainers on their kids' feet. An awful lot of ex-players suffer from depression or get divorced; they can't come to terms with the fact that the adulation isn't there anymore. So a lot of times they turn to substitutes to fill the gap in their lives where football used to be. It could be through gambling or drugs, or drinking – it happens to a lot of players and it's not their fault. They try these fixes because that's the only way they can get that slightly replicates the feeling of the 2.45pm adrenaline buzz in the dressing room before a game.

Ex-players need help and it should be coming from different sources. It should be the PFA, agents and ex-players who've been through difficult times who need to be coming back into football

LIFE AFTER FOOTBALL

not just as pundits or managers but running seminars, and talking about life skills and how to deal with life after football. Agents also need to take on a slightly different role: at the end of the day, the job of every agent is to get their player from 'A' to 'B' and get the maximum amount of money they can in every particular deal. OK, but agents should also be looking out for their players in a more holistic way. Too many agents basically lose interest when the earning potential goes down in a player's 30s then tails off completely. I would say that about 90 per cent of footballers don't even have a relationship with their agent by the time they hit 40 because the agents are busy with the new kids on the block. And often by then there's some bitterness or lack of communication. But that's exactly the age when ex-players need help the most. Money is short and they really need a lot of support and guidance.

To be fair, when you're a young player and everything is going your way, and somebody like me comes along and tries to warn you about the future, you don't want to hear it. But sometimes the players I tried to sit down with at the age of 29 or 30 come on the phone asking for help when they are 35. And at that point it's sometimes too late. Footballers need to understand that the game is a business. It's just a period of their life and around the age of 30 they need to start to prepare, and get people around them to help them develop new interests, make good investments, create business opportunities and new challenges so the minute they call it a day and retire they can thrust themselves into that. Being focused on your new life stops depression kicking in. Rio is a brilliant example of how to do this.

When I bumped into him again he was in his pomp, winning titles, playing in World Cups. Everyone knew about his footballing *ability but I saw another side to him and felt he was misunderstood. He was seen as unapproachable, a stereotypical footballer from the streets who'd made a lot of money and wasn't prepared to give anything back. I knew that wasn't true. He wanted to do a lot of things in the community; he wanted to be understood.*

You can see now how he's developed in the seven or eight years since then! I've seen him become a Dad with three little children; he's got married; I also saw him get a lot more serious in his approach to football.

In terms of preparation for life after football I think Rio is as happy as he could be when a lot of other footballers in his position are struggling. But he doesn't just want to make sure that he's happy in himself; he wants to work with me to raise this awareness among young players and help others. The way he sees it, if you stay strong and you believe in the people around you, collectively, you can achieve anything you want.

World Cup 2014

*Happy Mondays
And Tuesdays
And Wednesdays …*

Brazil

Brazil was my first World Cup as a fan rather than a player but I only got to see one game in person, Bosnia-Herzegovina v. Argentina. All the rest I watched on TV like most people! Pretty crazy, eh? But I was working for the BBC so I couldn't pick and choose. At the Maracanã, as soon as the national anthems started, the hairs on the back of my neck stood up and all I could think of was, 'I'd love to be playing!' The brilliant Argentina supporters were going mad and the atmosphere was unforgettable. But then all the South Americans were brilliant. Most nights I would walk along the Copacabana with my friend Jamie, just people-watching. I'd put my cap on and keep walking, hoping not to get recognised because I just wanted to drink in the occasion. The best-supported teams were Argentina,

Chile, Uruguay and Colombia, and their campervans were in all of the side and back streets, covered with flags. Fans had driven across the continent and every night were out partying, drinking and having sing-offs against each other.

The two most memorable moments of the tournament itself were the two biggest shocks: Spain getting hammered 5–1 by the Dutch in the first round, and Brazil collapsing 7–1 to Germany in the semi-final. Holland–Spain was the end of one era. Brazil–Germany, was the beginning of another. It was just crazy. Both times, in the studio, we just kept looking at each and saying, 'Are we really witnessing this?' I'd spoken to Ruud Gullit a couple of nights before the first game and, like everyone, he said Holland had no chance as their defence wasn't good enough. Then they went out and put on a performance like that! You just thought, 'Wow!' And then something even more astonishing happened. The host nation got destroyed in their own backyard. It was just surreal. Every time Brazil played a match the atmosphere in Rio was extraordinary. Up in the favelas on the mountains above Copacabana there would be gunshots and fireworks. Everyone was so excited. After the 7–1, I went out into the city expecting mayhem. But it was just very quiet and there was a sense of shock. All the people walking around seemed to be thinking: 'Did we really just see that? … We're going to wake up tomorrow … this can't be true.'

The two teams I enjoyed watching the most were Chile and Colombia. I especially liked the thrustful way Chile played. As soon as they won the ball, they went at their opponents. Meanwhile, Colombia had James Rodríguez, who I reckon is going to be the best player in the world within two or three years. He is the heir to the throne of Ronaldo and Messi and was just electrifying. Every time he got the ball he was looking to hurt the opposition with through balls, or making runs, committing people, shooting, setting up chances. And he's left-footed! Somehow, everything just looks better when you're left-footed. I said before the tournament that he'd be one to watch but I didn't expect him to be quite as good as he was. But other players you wanted to be brilliant never really rose to the occasion. Messi, Ronaldo and Neymar didn't quite do what we hoped they would do. But Thomas Müller was brilliant, as was the whole German team. Schweinsteiger, Kroos and Khedira were great and Neuer, their goalkeeper, was just unbelievable. I liked Cuadrado the right-midfielder for Colombia and Alexis Sánchez for Chile as well: exciting players doing exciting things for their countries.

Something else made a big impression on me. After I visited the England team following the Italy game, I went to the Dutch squad's hotel. The difference was so telling! The English had just lost so obviously they were a bit dejected. It's natural. Then I went to the Dutch team where I met Robin van Persie. Holland had just beaten Spain and everyone was smiling and Robin was laughing his head off, telling jokes, and talking about Louis van Gaal. He was saying, 'He tells us before the game, "this is how the game is going to play out" … and everything happens exactly as he predicts. He didn't say we were going to score five goals but he did tell us how we were going to win.' Robin was still bubbling after his amazing flying header goal. I asked him how he'd done it because normally you'd expect the striker to take a touch in that situation. He said it was pure instinct.

On the way back to our hotel I said to Jamie: 'That team is going to go deep in this tournament. They believe in the manager, in his ideas and philosophy. If he tells them the grass is blue, the grass is blue. If he tells them the sky is green, the sky is flipping green. They're going everywhere with him!' Another aspect that impressed me was that Van Gaal treated his players as grown-ups. One evening we were in a bar at the hotel with Fabio Cannavaro, waiting for Christian Vieri to come along. All of a sudden almost the entire Dutch team turn up and start chilling in this bar. I sat down next to Sneijder and said 'What's going on? Are you allowed in here?' He was like, 'Yeah, the manager said to go. As long as we're back in the hotel by 11, it's fine.' Me and Jamie just looked at each other and started laughing. Our players are treated like complete babies. It doesn't really matter whether that's because people have made mistakes in the past, or the manager doesn't trust the players or he doesn't trust the media who would make a story of it. I don't think the Dutch media even mentioned it. Their players looked free and relaxed: 'Yeah, we're out and we'll be back in a little while. It doesn't matter. We're not doing anything crazy.' I started thinking: this lot have got it sorted, tactically, technically and there's a great spirit in the team.

One of the best things about being at the tournament was the chance to meet legends like George Weah, Bakero, Pelé and Valderrama. And I loved going out for drinks and dinner with guys I'd played against over the years like Fabio

WORLD CUP 2014

Cannavaro, Christian Vieri, Clarence Seedorf and Thierry Henry. There was no competitive edge to them. We just chilled and relaxed and talked about good old times and the future of football. One conversation with Christian Vieri made a particular impression. He was known as a bit of a playboy in his time and he lives in Miami now. He said: 'I love my life now but I finished playing a year or two too early.' His advice to me was: play as long as you can, play till you feel you physically can't do it anymore. Others said the same thing. Shearer, Lineker, Keown and Seedorf said 'Just keep playing.' Ruud Gullit surprised me by telling me he had his most enjoyable time at the end of his career at Chelsea, who weren't a top team at the time. After his years in Italy the expectations and the pressure came off when he moved to London, and he just loved it there. He also put me right about Fabio Capello. I asked what it was like to play in that fantastic Milan team of the late 1980s and early 1990s and he said: 'But Capello didn't build that team – he *inherited* it from Arrigo Sacchi.' If I'd known that when he was England manager I would've been less disappointed.

Working for the BBC produced some surprises as well – all good ones. Going in, I hadn't realised just how good Gary Lineker was. But when I saw him up close everything about him, from the way he conducted himself, to the ad-libbing and writing his own scripts was just so impressive. A lot of what he does is structured, and he's got a good backup team, but he does a lot of it off the cuff and manages everything brilliantly. He's made the transition from being a top footballer to become a top man in another field. A lot of people don't know him as Gary Lineker the footballer, but as Gary Lineker, *Match of the Day* man, and Gary Lineker, Walker's Crisps man.

I already knew some of the other old players I was working with. I'd played with or against Danny Murphy, Phil Neville and Martin Keown. Robbie Savage used to live near me. I knew Clarence Seedorf and Thierry Henry as well. But the biggest surprise was Alan Shearer. I'd played with him about ten or 15 times for England, but I'd never had a conversation with him. He was the captain but it was Tony Adams who came over and went, 'Hope you're all right and if you need anything, come and see me.' I always found Alan Shearer a bit cold. I don't know what to expect, but he was one of the nicest people. He made me feel so welcome. He was relaxed and at ease with himself. We had a good few nights out, a good few beers. If I needed any help or advice, he was there, and I felt we worked well on TV together. In fact, the dynamics in the studio worked really well with everyone. The BBC people made it very comfortable for me. Alan Hansen was great too. Everyone knows how brilliant he's been but within the BBC walls, his foibles are famous too: he falls asleep quite a lot and people are always taking the mick out of him – but he gives as good as he gets.

It was his last tournament, so there was a party after the final, and everyone had to do a little piece to camera about him. I said: 'What a fantastic player, really good on the ball, silky, started attacks at the back, won loads, was a great leader, well-liked by his teammates, what a fantastic player, a legend … That's me. Now let's talk about Alan Hansen.' That got a nice little chuckle. Then we were having a few drinks in the hotel – until the barman shut the bar! So we all went down to one of the little shacks on the beach which sell alcohol and melon. There must have been about 30 or 40 BBC people and locals and there was a beat system, so I got out my Ipad and found myself DJ'ing for Alan Hansen's *Match of the Day* farewell party on the Copacabana! A nice bit of Oasis, Happy Mondays, Bob Marley, and everyone was singing and dancing along. It was brilliant.

I'd worked as a pundit before, for BT Sport, but this was the biggest football tournament of all. The whole nation was watching and football history was being made. But I never allowed myself to think like that. I didn't think '14 or 15 million people are watching.' I didn't let that get into my head. Instead, I treated it like I was sitting and talking as I would to my mates in the pub or at home. I didn't get nervous, but I approached each commentary as professionally as I would a match I was playing in. One crucial aspect was research. If you don't do your preparation, if you don't find out everything you can about teams, players and coaches, you leave yourself wide open. There's a lot more to the whole process than meets the eye of the viewer. Every morning at breakfast one of the directors of the show came to meet me and discussed the running order of the show, which players would I like to profile and so on. The whole thing was a good education, and the feedback I've had for my match-day work and for the *Rio in Rio* documentary I made was all very positive.

Early in the tournament I was doing a game every day, but once the group games were over and the number of games decreased all of a sudden you're getting a day off here and there.

That's when I got a chance to indulge a bit on the beach and go off and do the documentary to see what life is like in the favelas. We went into Santa Marta and it was an eye-opener to see how ordinary people there live. They're poor and there are open sewers down the little alleyways. But the people there feel strongly about the government's 'resettlement' plans. They were saying: 'Leave us alone. We don't want anything. We understand poverty. We know how to get along. We're happy. If you can give us infrastructure, fantastic. But if not, leave us alone. Don't come in and tear our favelas apart. We live here. We have history here.' These people have lived in these places for years and years with their families. And they are being taken out of there for no reason I can see other than money. The real estate there is the best real estate in the city. The favelas are up in the mountains so they have beautiful views over the sea. The people there were telling me the government has broken its promises. Money is not being spent on transport systems, hospitals and education for the kids. So where is it going? That's why they are upset. The process underway is called 'pacification'. The military will go in and control the drug barons and 'pacify' the favela. Sometimes the authorities go in and basically ransack the favela, take over homes and move the people to a different part of the city. Some of these people work nearby in the centre of Rio, and they're being moved to three or four hours away. It's ridiculous. They're much worse off after they are moved away from friends and family. Imagine someone coming into your front room and saying, 'Right, you got a week to get out, and by the way, where you're going is worse than here.'

WORLD CUP 2014

England after Brazil

I had a memorable time in Brazil. I met some great people, and I'd love to go back. Waking up on the Copacabana beach every morning, you can't ask for much more than that, can you? Unfortunately, you could have asked for quite a bit more from England in the tournament. Our early exit as bottom team in our group, beaten by Italy and Uruguay, and with just one point from three games reminded us that something is fundamentally wrong in our national game. If it isn't fixed we'll be also-rans forever.

At one level, I thought we missed an opportunity to give youth its head. If Roy Hodgson had said at the outset: 'This is the tournament for the young players. We're not expecting to win the World Cup but we are preparing for the 2016 Euros and I want to give the kids experience. Win, lose or draw, as long as I see progress, it will be a good World Cup for us …' If he'd done that, maybe we would be able to go into the next tournament with more optimism. In England's first match against Italy it was exciting to see young players like Raheem Sterling, Ross Barkley, Danny Welbeck and Daniel Sturridge playing without fear. Raheem Sterling looked like he could win us the game. But then we got caught at the back and it fell apart. I was disappointed that in the second two games we didn't see any progress.

But even looking at the tournament like that is taking a short-term approach. The problems in our game that need to be addressed go much deeper. We have to be thinking about the Under 14s and 15s as the Germans and other top countries do. There are cycles in football and we need to create one of our own. Look at the Dutch. Going into the tournament, they were the least fancied of the bigger nations but they ended up a penalty shootout away from the final. That all stems from a Dutch philosophy developed over many years which puts an emphasis on technical excellence and passing. The Dutch performances were directly linked to their football history and tradition. Maybe their football wasn't as easy on the eye this time as it has been in the past. But it was still clearly in line with their ideas about youth development, coaching and tactical doctrines. They've been clever and clear-sighted about their football for decades and we need to create something like that for ourselves.

In England, people at the top of the game have to come together and agree to create our own philosophy of football to benefit the players we produce. We don't need to have an inferiority complex towards any football nation. We've got players who are as quick and as strong and able as anybody. Technically we have some good players but they need to be put in a system that works and which everyone understands and adheres to. At the moment, players have to go from Under 15s, 16s, 17s, 18s, 19s, 20s, 21s, to the first team and every coach at every level is doing something different. The FA is trying to make changes but the approach is nowhere near radical enough.

Look at the world champions. In Germany, over the last 15 years or so the clubs and the German FA have worked together on youth development and tactical systems because they all understand and agree that this benefits the players, and this in turn benefits the clubs and the national team. We don't see things that way. The Premier League is completely detached from the ideas and the vision of the FA and vice versa. The barrier has to be broken down. The big clubs have very little interest in the national team. All they care about is what benefits them, and they think mainly in terms of money. Each club develops its own identity and its own way of playing with no thought as to how it might fit with the national team. And the FA is not strong enough to decide on a policy and dictate from the centre. So what I expect will happen is what has always happened in English football. We'll muddle along, tweaking a few things here and there. You don't get results like that. You've got to be willing to upset a few people at the beginning but get people to buy into a long-term vision and wait for the fruits to grow. There are no short-term easy fixes.

We haven't got enough facilities and good coaches at all levels and opportunities for the best young players to get experience playing at the highest level. The reason I joined Greg Dyke's FA Commission was to travel and talk to people and learn more about what other countries are doing. The commission was always planning to issue two reports. The first got hammered for suggesting the creation of a new league to give young players at the top clubs more experience. But our intention was always to open the debate and I think it did that. Another report on more technical matters comes next, and we'll concentrate on some very specific problems we have compared to other countries.

For example, in the whole of England there are just 639 3G all-weather pitches. Germany has more than 5,000. An FA survey of clubs at all levels found 84 per cent of respondents saying that facilities are poor. This directly affects how many teams and at what age-groups kids can play. We have too few coaches, and those we have are not as well qualified as they should be. Spain has 25,000 coaches with A, B and Pro Licences. Germany has 35,000. We have 6,000. Coaching is respected elsewhere and is more highly-valued. In Germany and the Netherlands a youth coach can earn £40,000 a year. It's a profession. In England the equivalent pay is £16,000. That's a hobby. There's a clear link between these factors and the quality of the national team.

Another part of our problem is cultural. We've got far too many coaches who tell talented young players how to play rather than letting them develop naturally. In other countries, everything's about developing skills, touch, awareness. All I heard on the sidelines when I was growing up was about hard work and tackling. A good tackle would be applauded as much, if not more, than a great bit of skill. Tackling is a great part of the game. But, for me, the skill factor overrides everything else. The best players have the best skills because it's something they've done all their lives in their own, original, unstructured ways. Look at Cristiano Ronaldo: unstructured street football as a kid. He just played and played because he loved to play. The Brazilian Ronaldo, Maradona, Wayne Rooney, Franck Ribéry … all these guys are street footballers and originals who did things their way.

I've often spoken about this with Wayne and Cristiano. Wayne told me a few times how coaches wanted him to play in one position and he refused, saying 'No, I want to play here, because I'm the best and that's what I'm doing.' With guys like that, from a young age they've got their own ideas and they understand football and they know what they're good at. Unfortunately, some coaches see that as a threat and won't embrace it. At Everton, they left Wayne pretty much alone. They didn't try to beat it out of him, but other clubs at other times might have done. Everton were wise enough to know they had someone with the potential to be a top player; they embraced that and let him flourish and grow.

I always talk and tweet about philosophy. What is the English football philosophy these days? I don't even think we've got one. It's still mostly about running a hundred miles an hour and working hard. For any footballer working hard should be a given. I don't understand why you even get praised for hard work by itself. People pay to come and watch so the least you could do is put in a bit of effort. What you need is hard work within a good structure and a good philosophy.

At the same time, when you get good individual coaches at top clubs who have a clear idea of what they want, things can change fast. Look how quickly Roberto Martinez turned Everton away from being a team that liked to get the ball in the box from the back or from wide areas to being a possession side good enough to pass Arsenal off the pitch at the Emirates. Brendan Rodgers completely transformed Liverpool in a season. That's a different model: start at the top and hope it filters down to the Under 21s, 19s, 18s and all the different age groups. Maybe it can be done like that. But I can't see the whole country adopting one club or one manager's philosophy, however successful. A unified approach has to come from the very top. We need a clear direction and leadership. We're producing good players. But what's the point if no one knows how they can be fitted into the national team in a coherent way? What's the point? I'd rather have a team like Costa Rica who over-achieve with players not deemed to be world class.

Coming Home

Money has never been my motivation

I knew I wanted to keep playing after I left Man United – but I didn't know where. I had offers from clubs all over the world, many of them in places with beautiful climates. Premier League clubs wanted me too. I wasn't sure what to do until I got a phone call from Harry Redknapp. Then everything became clear.

Places in Asia and the Gulf and America are great to visit on holiday. But would I really want to live and work there? I wasn't sure. The more I thought about it, the more I realised I wanted to come home. I'm a London boy at heart. I made great friends in Manchester and I'll always stay in touch with them. But London is where my family and oldest friends are. Added to that, I want my kids to get to know London and I've just built a house 15 minutes from the city by train.

In the middle of all this, Harry called and asked me to join him at QPR. Harry Redknapp. My first gaffer. A man I respect greatly. The manager who did so much to help me when I was starting. Suddenly my mind was made up. I realised that if I didn't play in London I didn't really want to go on playing anywhere. I'd simply retire. Harry said at a press conference soon after I signed that my wages were 'incredibly low' but I didn't see it that way. It's true that I could have got double, triple or quadruple elsewhere. But I've never been motivated by money. I never get out of bed thinking 'How much money am I going to earn today?' I get up thinking, 'What am I going to achieve today?' The way I see it is that I've earned well during my career. I always believed that if I played well, then I was paid well. But the last thing I'd want would be to come to QPR and take liberties. The club has had that experience over the last few years with too-generous deals handed out to players. I didn't want to be tarred with that brush.

Harry and the London connection weren't the only attractions. I have loads of history with QPR. In fact the whole family does. My brother Anton played for QPR and my cousin Les played there. And it was my first club. When I was 11 or 12 I played a cup game for my uncle Dave's team Bloomfield Athletic. A QPR scout called Sandy was there to see our opponents, Long Lane. But he ended up taking three or four from my team, including me. That led to me training at QPR for a couple of years, mostly with a terrific coach called Paul Haversham. One of the things I used to enjoy about the club was that we got free tickets to see the first team play. And they had good players like Ray Wilkins, Clive Wilson and Alan McDonald. After a while, as I explained in 'Frankly', Frank Lampard Senior persuaded me to join West Ham and the rest is history. But I always had fond memories of QPR because I had a good time there. One of my mates at that time was Nigel Quashie who was a year older than me, but came from the same area.

When I was a teenager at West Ham, Harry Redknapp gave me the confidence to go out, be myself and try anything on the field. He gave me freedom and convinced me I was going to be a first-team player. He had a unique style for giving compliments. In the changing room, he'd talk to someone else – but make sure I could hear! He might be talking to one of the coaches and say of me: 'He's that skinny, but he's gonna be some player, I'm tellin' you!' One time I'd had a stinker against Luton and after the game he was in the middle of the changing room talking to one of the coaches, going: 'There's nothing of him, look, nothing of him! But what a fucking player! He's so fast. He's some talent!' A week later he sent me out on loan to Bournemouth. I was reluctant at the time but he said: 'You go there, and when you come back you'll be ready for the first team,' and he was true to his word.

His friend, Mel Machin, was the manager there and he was similar to Harry. I was a bit nervous going into training the first time but afterwards, in front of a few of the guys in the corridor, he said to me: 'I'm going to call you "Class" from now on! That's your name. Class!' That gave me so much confidence. I was only there two months and played 12 games but I made some good friends there and had good times and still keep in touch with some of the players like Jason Brissett. But it was all part of Harry's plan to get me some experience. When I came back to London he put me in the first team straightaway and I never looked back. I don't think some managers realise just how important it can be to encourage young players. Just a little comment can do so much good. For example, when Terry Venables was England manager I went, as a kid, just to train with the team during Euro 96. I walked past him after a training session and he said, 'Oh, you were magnificent today, son.' You go back to your room and your hairs on the back of your neck are standing up and you ring all your mates and say, 'Terry Venables the England manager just said I was unbelievable. I must have a chance of getting in the squad!'

Harry encouraged all the skilful players. He loved them, embraced them. You'd hear him in training with Joe Cole: 'Oh Coley! What have we got here? He's a *magician*!' Any piece of skill. He loved it. That's what he used to say to me, 'Don't worry about mistakes. Make mistakes. Just don't make the same ones over and over. I wanna see you do what you do. You're brilliant … ' We used to do one-on-ones all the time at West Ham, and he made me go against Paolo di Canio all the time … and you'd hear him: 'Go on Paolo! Go on Paolo! Beat 'im! Beat 'im!' He'd be winding you up, but in a nice way.

It's important for managers to give their young players confidence – but they also have to know when to bring them back down to earth. Harry was brilliant at that too. It's lovely that he's still got all his old enthusiasm. My only reservation, looking back, was that at West Ham in the 1990s there was always a low expectation about winning trophies. That was more to do with the older players and the drinking culture, but the mentality was all about just avoiding relegation. If we'd had more of a winning mentality we could have gone on to do more at the club. And maybe if I'd had more of that mentality earlier in my career I could have gone further and achieved more. But Harry gave me a good platform to start from. He loved players to express themselves and, unlike some managers, he would never punish you for making mistakes on the field if you were trying to create something. So I grew up without fear of playing. A lot of players I know didn't have that.

Harry's disciplinary style was certainly unique. Whenever I was in trouble – it was never serious, but it did happen occasionally – he would call me into his office and point to the giant picture of Bobby Moore behind his desk almost the size of the whole wall. Harry would say: 'Do you think *he* would do what you did? Would he have got himself in these situations? I played with that guy! That's who you've got to live up. You've got a long road but you've got the potential to do something in this game. Look at him! What would he have done? Think about that!' He was always talking about Bobby Moore and referring back to him.

He doesn't have that picture above his desk at QPR but in a way the club is similar to West Ham back then. It's like I've come back to my roots. In fact it's almost as if I've stepped into a time machine. The one obvious difference between the QPR training ground at Harlington and Manchester United's Carrington is money. United spent millions and millions of pounds on their facilities. But I like the kind of rustic, old-school feel. I've known the QPR training ground since I was a kid. It's got the evocative old smell. It's got memories. Obviously, there's nothing here like Man United's swimming pool. But it's not something that I thumb my nose at, it's just different. We've got the basics, and that's all you need as a footballer. We've got everything we need to make sure that we're ready to go out and play football on a Saturday.

Another delight is working with Glenn Hoddle again. When he took his first coaching session I just couldn't stop smiling. He was teaching us how to play three-at-the back and move without the ball to open up spaces for others to exploit. He explains things as well as anyone I have worked with. And then he did something casually brilliant that took me back to when I was 18 and training under him with England. There was a long kick from the goalkeeper and he plucked the ball out of the sky with the outside of his foot and carried on talking as if it was nothing! I just burst out laughing aloud because I remembered him doing exactly the same thing when he was the England manager: killing a high ball dead without even breaking his train of thought. What touch! What poise! What nonchalance!

As to my role, I'm not planning to go in saying this or that. Actions speak louder than anything else and if people want to take on board my work ethic, and the way that I play, my attitude and the information I can give, then great. Harry knows what I bring and he hasn't got to tell me to do things. If I see something and I think something needs saying, I'll say it. But I'm lucky. I've come into a good changing room, with a good bunch of lads who all want to do well. And some of them I've known for years. Joey Barton, obviously, is a big tweeter like myself. I know Danny Simpson from when he was at Man United as a kid. I've played against and with Bobby Zamora, Rob Green and Jermaine Jenas over the years.

COMING HOME

It's a different type of pressure from what I was used to at Manchester United. But the pressure will still be on and I'm looking forward to seeing how I cope with that and how it affects me in different ways. Naturally, the first fixture I looked for was when we play United. When I saw it was the fourth game of the season, I automatically started working it out: 'Yeah, it's going to be hard, and they're a good team, and I'll be up against all my mates, and 0–0 would be a good result, but beating them would be even better.'

Harry helped me a lot when I was young. He gave me confidence and he believed in me. This season I'd like to help him. To finish off my career together again is like coming full circle. How will the story end? Hopefully, QPR can survive and stay in the Premier League. That would be a happy ending. That would be a *great* ending!

Index

#5 184, 186, 226
50 Cent 168, 184
'99 Treble 28

AC Milan 66, 79, 197
Accrington Stanley 156
Aguero, Sergio 136
Akon 168
Alam, Faria 78
Alonso, Xabi 190
Anderson, Viv 47, 85, 162
Anelka, Nicolas 86–7
Anfield 48, 178
Anya (sister) v, 217
apartheid 45, 58, 70
Apple 87
Arsenal 25, 26, 29, 31, 46, 94, 113–14, 159, 192, 199, 209, 255
Arteta, Mikel 95
AS Roma 80, 225
Asian tour 131, 187, 257
Aston Villa 139
Atlético Madrid 143, 224

Bakero, Jose Maria 246
Bale, Gareth 213
ballet 107, 108, 109
Barcelona ('Barça') 92, 98, 111–18, 189, 226

Baresi, Franco 80
Barkley, Ross 251
Barnes, John 2, 3, 47, 69, 70, 162, 207, 226
Barnsley 194
Barry, Gareth 76
Barton, Joey 262
basketball 176
Batson, Brendon 47
Bayern Munich 35, 97, 140–1, 142–3, 144
BBC 187, 243, 247, 248–9
Beckham, David ('Becks') 17, 28, 29, 77, 95, 131, 189, 197, 205
Bellamy, Craig 93, 177
Benfica 95
Benzema, Karim 213
Berbatov, Dimitar ('Berba') 92, 96, 97
Bergkamp, Dennis 179–80
Bernard (cousin) 200
Best, Clyde 48
Best, George 117, 131, 182
Bexley and Kent League 149
Billy Elliot 108
Blackberry Clinic 42
Blackheath Bluecoats 6
Blackheath District 193
Blatter, Sepp 66–7
Bloomfield Athletic 258

INDEX

Boateng, Kevin Prince 66
Boca Juniors 99
Bolt, Usain 186
Bolton Wanderers 29, 100, 198
Bournemouth 9, 237, 259
Bowen, Justin 6
Bowyer, Lee 124
boxing 209
Brasingamens 100
Brown, Wes 29, 158
Bruce, Steve 116
BT Sport 249
Bullard, Jimmy 149–50
Burgess Park 3
Burnley 25
Burrows, Frank 15
Busby Babes 86, 117
Busby, Matt 31
Busquets, Sergio 113, 227
Butt, Nicky 16, 28

Campbell, Sol 163
Cannavaro, Fabio 246–7
Capello, Fabio 79–82, 125, 150, 151, 247
Cardiff 13
Carling Cup 23, 24
Carlisle 9
Carlisle, Clark 62
Carr, Tony 8, 194
Carragher, Jamie 80
Carrick, Michael 3, 16, 28, 84, 85, 94, 172, 200
Carrington 18, 144, 261
Carroll, Andy 134
Cartwright, John 47
Celtic 31, 162, 178
Champions' League, 23–5, 28, 35, 86, 88, 90, 111, 114, 115, 126, 140, 165, 178–9, 183, 200, 224–5
Chapman, Tracy 167, 168
Charlton Athletic 47, 162, 206
Charlton, Bobby 87, 88, 117, 120

Chelsea 12, 25–6, 31, 50, 53–4, 85–7, 140, 197–9, 206, 247
Chicarito 28, 139
Chloe (sister) v, 217
'choc ice' tweet 56, 59, 68
Cleverley, Tom 28
Clough, Brian 129
Club World Cup Championship 126
Coker, Ade 48
Cole, Ashley 53, 54–5, 56–7, 84, 86, 87, 150, 199, 200
Cole, Joe 3, 86, 260
community football 231
Coppell, Steve 131
Costa Rica 256
Cottee, Tony 6–7
Crewe Alexandra 237
Crouch, Peter 133
Crown Prosecution Service (CPS) 53
Crystal Palace 30
Cuadrado, Juan 245

Dave (uncle) 258
Davies, Kevin 18, 180
Dead Man Running 230
Deco 112
Delap, Rory 133
depression 41, 42, 236, 237, 240, 241
Derby County 47
di Canio, Paolo 37, 260
discrimination 68; *see also* gay footballers; racism
divorce 216–17, 240
DJ Luck 168
dog racing 152
Dowie, Ian 200
Drake 168
Drogba, Didier 31, 86, 101
Duberry, Michael 124
Dublin, Dion 13, 180
Dyke, Greg 253

Eltham Town 149

INDEX

Emirates 255
Eriksson, Sven-Göran 77
Eto'o, Samuel 113
Euro 96 260
Euro 2008 78
Euro 2012 53, 60, 84
Euro 2016 251
European Championships 76, 81, 112
European Cup 31, 197
Evans, Jonny 172
Everton United 37, 128–9, 130, 135, 138–9, 144, 255
Evra, Patrice ('Pat') 28, 29, 48–9, 50, 99, 143

FA Cup 13, 25, 89, 197
Fabio, Don 79
Fàbregas, Cesc 95
Facebook 187
Farrell, Andy 103
Fashanu, Justin 121
Federer, Roger 185–6
Ferdinand, Anton (brother) v, 14, 45, 50–1, 52–9, 61–2, 70, 71, 87, 99, 157, 162, 217, 238, 258
Ferdinand, Jeremiah (brother) v, 14, 45, 157, 217
Ferdinand, Les (cousin) 13, 19, 180, 258
Ferdinand, Lorenz v
Ferdinand, Rebecca (wife) v, 14, 217–19
Ferdinand, Tate v
Ferdinand, Tia v
Ferguson, Alex ('Fergie') v, 18, 26, 31, 40, 61, 91–102, 108, 128, 129, 132–3, 136, 138–40, 167
Ferguson, Duncan 13, 35, 180, 184, 225, 226
FIFA 66
Fletcher, Darren 16, 28, 155, 156, 158, 172
Football Association (FA) 48–9, 51–55, 59, 67–8, 71, 89, 209, 253–4
Fortune, Quinton ('Quinny') 224
Foster, Ben 23–4, 30–1
Foxx, Jamie 186, 187
Friary Estate 4
Fulham 134, 149

Gascoigne, Paul ('Gazza') 3, 226
gay footballers 68, 119–21
German FA 252
Gerrard, Steven ('Stevie') 81, 82, 84, 95, 101, 197
Giggs, Ryan ('Giggsy') 16, 17, 28, 29, 34, 85–6, 88, 90, 96, 125–6, 130, 131, 141, 145, 159, 172, 191
Gill, David 42, 147
Gill, Oliver ('Ollie') 156
Grandstand 2
Green, Rob 161
Guardiola, Pep 112, 117, 143
Gullit, Ruud 80, 244, 247
Guns N' Roses 168
gymnastics 107, 109
Gyptian 169

Hamilton, Lewis 187
Hansen, Alan 248, 249
Happy Mondays 249
Hargreaves, Owen 16, 29, 85
Harlington 261
Hart, Joe 199
Haversham, Paul 258
Henry, Thierry 29, 48, 113, 179, 189, 199, 226–7, 247, 248
Hernández, Javier ('Chicarito') 28, 139
Hernández, Xavi 113, 116, 179, 189, 213, 227
Heskey, Emile 203, 234
Highbury Park 159
Hillsborough 30
Hitchcock, Kevin 31

INDEX

Hitzlsperger, Thomas 119, 121
Hoddle, Glenn 73, 74–6, 77, 84, 151, 262
Hodgson, Roy 60, 61, 83–4, 251
horse racing 152, 153
Hughes, Mark 19, 93
Hughton, Chris 162
Hull City 25, 149

Ibrahimovic, Zlatan 213
Ince, Paul 3, 47, 48, 162
inclusion 68
Iniesta, Andrés 113, 116, 179, 189, 227
Inter Milan 23, 114, 190

Jagielka, Phil 134
James, David 17
Januzaj, Adnan 8, 169
Jay-Z 168, 169
Jenas, Jermaine 262
Johnson, Glen 3

Kagawa, Shinji 28, 143
Kallaghan 168
Kano 168
Keane, Robbie 124
Keane, Roy 16, 28, 29, 127, 155–60, 205
Keegan, Kevin 76
Keith, Joe 8
Kelly, Gary 124
Kenyon, Peter 205–6
Keown, Martin 199, 247, 248
Khedira, Sami 245
Kick It Out 48, 52, 62–7
Kidd, Brian 138
King, Martin Luther 58
Kolarov, Aleksanda 137
Kroos, Toni 190, 245

Lampard, Frank Jr 3, 8, 77, 78, 86, 95, 101, 152, 193–201

Lampard, Frank Sr 193, 195, 196, 258
Lampard, Patricia 195
Latchford, Bob 225
Law, Denis 117
League Cup 30, 156
Leeds United 12, 15, 16, 27, 123, 124, 129, 157, 179, 198
Lewin, Gary 203
Lidlow, Kevin 35
Lil Wayne 168
Lindegaard, Anders 144
Lineker, Gary 247, 248
Lisa (Dad's partner) v, 216, 217
Liverpool 2, 29, 30, 33, 48, 49, 101, 135, 140, 156–7, 178, 255
London Games 107
Lorenz (friend) 87
Lumsden, Jimmy 144
Luton Town 259
Lynch, Danny 62

Mc Neat 168
McAnally, Dr 42
McDonald, Alan 258
McFarlane, Andy 6
Machin, Mel 259
McLaren, Steve 78–9
Maldini, Paolo 80
Manchester City 25, 26, 31–2, 129, 135, 136, 178, 191, 214
Manchester United 8–9, 16, 20, 23, 25–31, 39, 48, 49, 59, 78, 79, 83, 85, 86, 92, 95, 117, 119, 123–5, 127–30, 135, 138–9, 141–2, 144, 146–7, 157–8, 165, 167, 170, 172, 175, 182, 189–90, 198, 200–1, 205–8, 211, 216, 222, 224, 226, 235, 237, 257, 261–3
Manchester United TV 158–60
Mandela, Nelson 58, 70
Mandžukic, Mario 142
Maradona, Diego 2, 3, 254
Marley, Bob 168, 249

INDEX

Martinez, Roberto 255
Mata, Juan 8, 169, 213
Match of the Day 2, 12, 248, 249
Meredith, Billy 131
Messi, Lionel 113, 115–17, 179, 213, 221–7, 245
Metropolitan Police five-a-sides 27
Meulensteen, Rene 138
Millwall 46, 47
Mitten, Charlie 131
MK Dons 162
Moore, Bobby 196, 261
Moore, Darren 67
Moralee, Jamie vi, 61–2, 200, 204, 237–9, 243, 246
Morgan, Albert 64, 167
Morgan, Piers 209
Morgan, Willie 131
Morris, Jody 200, 204, 237
Mourinho, José 92, 114, 198
Moyes, David 127, 128–36, 138–44, 146–7, 171
Müller, Thomas 142, 245
Munich air disaster 30, 31, 86
Murphy, Danny 248
Murs, Olly 187, 230

Nani 28, 29, 85, 93
Nasri, Samir 137
Nastasić, Matija 137
Nesbitt, James 233
Neuer 245
Neville, Gary 16, 29, 96, 97–8, 125, 126, 129
Neville, Phil 248
New Era vi, 184, 186, 188, 239
Newcastle United 23, 93, 141, 162, 214
Neymar 2, 245
NFL 176
N'n'G 168
Norwich City 145, 162
Notorious B.I.G. 168

Oasis 188, 249
Old Trafford 1, 99, 102, 114–15, 140, 165
O'Leary, David 12, 123
Olympiacos 140
One Direction 230
One Game, One Community 63
O'Shea, John ('Sheasy') 28, 156, 158
Ouseley, Lord 68
Owen, Michael 13, 75

P. Diddy 183
Park, Ji-Sung 8, 29, 113
Parris, George 48
Pedro 116, 117
Pegg, David 131
Pelé 246
Peter (Mum's partner) v, 216–17
'Peter Pan' lifestyle 236
PFA 62, 129, 240
Phelan, Mick 129
Piqué, Gerard 102
Pirlo, Andrea 84, 190, 213
Player of the Year 189, 223
Porto 225
Postman Pat 150
Powell, Chris 162
Power, Keith 17
Premier League 20, 24–5, 81–2, 90, 128, 140, 156, 144, 161, 162, 178, 189, 214, 226, 239, 253, 257, 263
Prince's Trust 229–30
Professional Footballers Association (PFA) 62, 129, 240
Puyol, Carles 227

Q&As 208
Quashie, Nigel 259
Queens Park Rangers (QPR) vii, 10, 31, 50, 236, 257–8, 261, 263
Queiroz, Carlos 18, 88, 138, 211–12

INDEX

racism 45–71, 84, 161
Radebe, Lucas 123–4
Raúl 17, 179
Ray (friend) 87, 200
Real Madrid 80, 88, 118, 224
Redknapp, Harry v, vii, 194, 196, 235–6, 257–63
Remy (sister) v, 217
RESPECT 66
retirement 35, 37, 40, 80, 93, 236, 239–40, 241, 258
Ribéry,, Franck 254
Ridsdale, Peter 12
Rijkaard, Frank 3, 80, 112
Rio Ferdinand Foundation 229–34
Rio in Rio 249
Ritchie Barbers 234
Rivaldo 13, 14
Roberts, Jason 64, 67
Robinson, Paul 13, 79
Rock, Chris 234
Rodgers, Brendan 255
Rodríguez, James 244–5
Ronaldinho 112, 225, 227
Ronaldo 13, 14, 227
Ronaldo, Cristiano 17, 28, 85, 88, 95–6, 113, 114, 120, 131, 157, 169, 213, 221–7, 245, 254
Rooney, Wayne 17, 20, 28, 77, 95, 97, 114, 120, 143, 172, 199, 211–14, 230, 254,
Rose, Gavin 2, 3, 87, 200, 238
Rosso 182
Round, Steve 144
Rourke, Mickey 186
Ruddock, Neil 19
rugby 36, 103, 104, 152, 209

Sacchi, Arrigo 247
Saha, Louis 17, 18, 20, 39
Saint and Greavsie 2
Sánchez, Alexis 245
Savage, Robbie 248

Scherzinger, Nicole 187
Scholes, Paul ('Scholesy') 16, 18, 28–9, 94, 169, 172, 189–92, 197
Schweinsteiger, Bastian 245
Scottish Premier League 156
Seedorf, Clarence 247, 248
Shankly, Bill 31
Shearer, Alan 12, 180, 247, 248
Shittu, Danny 178
Show Racism The Red Card 48, 67
Sian (sister) v, 217
Simeone, Diego 143
Simpson, Danny 262
Sky 126, 192
Smalling, Chris 142
Smith, Pete vi, 184
Smith, Will 186
Sneijder, Wesley 246
Solskjaer, Ole Gunnar 17, 214
Southampton United 29, 235
Spring Gardens 181
Stannett, Gary 232
Stefan (friend) 2
Stein, Jock 31
Sterling, Raheem 234, 251
Stewart, Michael 156
Stoke City 34, 64, 133, 139
Stone Roses 167, 168
Sturridge, Daniel 251
Suárez, Luis 48–50, 59, 66, 69, 99, 213
Sugar Lounge 100
Sunderland United 31, 32
Swansea City 64, 102

T-Pain 168
Tempah, Tinie 187
Terry, John 50–1, 53–6, 60, 67–71, 78, 81, 84, 85–7, 99, 125, 150, 162, 199
Tevez, Carlos 28, 85, 99, 114
Three Champions' League 28
tiki-taka 92, 113, 117

270

INDEX

Torres, Fernando 33, 177
Tottenham Hotspurs 23, 92
Toure, Yaya 227
Tournoi de France 76
Twitter 51, 56, 59, 66, 68, 172, 186–7, 204–5, 207–8, 255, 262

unemployment 240
U2 168
Usher 208

Valderrama, Carlos 246
Valencia, Antonio 93
van Basten, Marco 80
van der Sar, Edwin 29, 86–7, 115
van Gaal, Louis 91, 146, 214, 245–6
van Nistelrooy, Ruud 17, 20, 28, 156, 157, 222–3
van Persie, Robin 26, 28, 94, 172, 213, 245
Venables, Terry 260
Verón, Ricardo 28
Vidić, Nemanja 20, 21, 28, 29, 86–8, 102, 115–17, 126, 133, 136–7, 169, 172, 200
Vieira, Patrick 159–60, 189, 199
Vieri, Christian 246–7
Villa, David 116

WAGs 219
Watford 178, 238, 211
Weah, George 246
Welbeck, Danny 28, 143, 251
Wembley 1, 111, 115
Wenger, Arsène 209

West Ham vii, 3, 6, 11, 12, 15, 16, 19, 27, 37, 48, 74, 139, 149, 157, 171, 178, 193, 194, 198, 200, 214, 229, 236, 258–61
West, Kanye 168
Westminster Magistrates' Court 55
Wigan 64, 125, 126, 149
Wilkins, Ray 10, 186, 258
Wilkinson, Howard 76
Wilshere, Jack 192
Wilson, Clive 258
Wimbledon 185
Wolfart, Muller 35
women's football 68
Woodgate, Jonathan 124
Woodward, Ed 235
World Championships 76
World Cup 13, 15, 58, 73, 76, 81, 84, 124–6, 187, 203–5, 226, 241, 243–56
World Player of the Year 223
World Youth Championships 2
Wright, Ian 162, 177
Wright-Phillips, Shaun 150

Y-Tribe 168
Yeovil 9
YMCA 149
Young, Ashley 28
YouTube 2, 14, 51, 190

Zahavi, Pini vi, 205, 237
Zamora, Bobby 262
Zidane, Zinédine 179, 189, 227

Rio: My Decade as a Red (ISBN: 9781743469880).
Available from all good book retailers.